What

Networking on Purpose
Five-Part Networking Success Plan™

"This book is short, it's easy-to-read, and it is packed with so many nuggets of golden wisdom that you'll be able to use it as your ongoing guide for successful networking for as long as you're in business."

> – Bob Burg, Co-author of *The Go-Giver* and Author of *Endless Referrals*

"Beth has personally used her strategies to build a strong viable network. If you follow the Five Part Networking Success Plan™ you, too, can build a network that will serve you well. If you're a business owner, business executive, manager or employee, a student, or a solo-prenuer, 'Networking on Purpose ' is a must read."

> – Robert Mano, CEO: Mano Y Mano Consulting LLC, Consultant/Speaker Author; "Thinking Beyond the Obvious – a simple concept that drives business success." www.thinkingbeyondtheobvious.com

"Beth Bridges is the foremost expert on business networking in the chamber industry. That is saying something because chambers are all about relationships and networking. If you want to improve your ability when it comes to business networking, you can't find a better resource than Beth. Listen to her."

> – Frank J. Kenny, Owner and Author, Frank J. Kenny, LLC, FrankJKenny.com

"I have grown my businesses, found incredible mentors and made even my roughest jobs run more smoothly by using Beth's Five-Part Networking Success Plan™ to fine-tune my personal and business network. I've leveraged existing relationships and expanded my network in a way I never thought possible. 'Networking on Purpose' is a guide for every small business owner no matter what industry you are in."

– Brett Taylor, Owner, Taylor Design,
  www.taylorhomedesign.com

"If you're building a direct sales or marketing business, you need to know the Five-Part Networking Success Plan™ and how to apply it. Beth is an expert networker, an incredible businesswoman and outstanding person. She has made networking easy for everyone to understand and implement. I've been applying these ideas to my own successful network marketing business. 'Networking on Purpose' showed me where I can fine-tune my strategy, focus more and succeed even faster."

– Mary Swarts, Senior Manager, SendOutCards,
  www.cardsfromyourpc.com

"Beth Bridges hits the nail on the head about networking with a concise, readable, and comprehensive overview of the principles every networker needs to master. Her insight is tested, practical, and transferable. Her suggestions will spark any active imagination to action. Be prepared to take notes manually and mentally because this is a ride you will want to return to again and again. This book is a basic manual that you will keep on your desk and refer to for years. Get multiple copies to give away and you are sure to make many friends who will be deeply indebted to you. If you are interested in success in networking, this is the book."

– Tom Sims, Pastor, Coach, Author, Encourager,
http://pastortomsims.com

"I can count on one hand the people who truly understand 'networking.' Beth Bridges is one of them. We all network, from hip tech startup founders to Fortune 500 CEOs, but most are rotten at it. Purposeful networking separates the successful from the failing business person and entrepreneur. Networking is about giving value, and I've built my business on this model. I know that serving them first means selling them later. 'Networking on Purpose' will help you learn this and more to leverage the power of networking."

– Todd Schnick, CEO, The Intrepid Group, LLC,
Business Talk Show Host

"As a leading Transformational Coach, I see people hanging back all the time. Beth will help you transform ordinary networking events into powerful opportunities to build your business, improve your life, and help others while you're at it—win, win, win!"

– Jill Hendrickson, Transformational Coach
Extraordinaire, www.JillHendrickson.com

"As America's Business Etiquette Coach, I know that networking is a missing key for many professionals. Often they misunderstand the true essence of the ebb and flow of networking. This critical skill is necessary for any professional. 'Networking on Purpose' is a must-read to feel confident both personally and professionally."

– Dallas Teague Snider, America's Business Etiquette
Coach & Impression Engineer,
www.makeyourbestimpression.com

"It had to be fate ... or networking! Beth has been an inspiration since she sat by me at a writers conference five years ago. She taught me that it's all about making a connection, staying connected, and preparing for future connections in all that we do. Her book will do the same for you. In 'Networking on Purpose,' Beth passionately captures the key elements which will help you navigate your way to networking success."

– Denise Lee Branco, Award-Winning Author of Horse at the Corner Post: Our Divine Journey, www.HorseAtTheCornerPost.com

"Nervous about networking? Here's a straightforward plan of action for you. This book clearly lays out why growing my network is important. I now have an essential reference manual to guide and improve how I and my team give and receive value in the marketplace. This is what every young business person and entrepreneur needs to know to confidently grow and work with the people they know and the people they will meet."

– Carlos Camerena, Entrepreneur, www.CarlosC.net

"'Networking on Purpose' is a wonderful, practical how-to guide for everyone who wants to be successful! Beth Bridges does a beautiful job outlining the how and whys of this important art form. If you are a new professional or someone who wants to 'go to the next level' - this book is for you!"

– Betsy A. Hays, Speaker, Author & Educator, www.BetsyHaysPR.com

"As a young professional in finance, my career took me to a new city. The networking strategies that Beth has taught me have been incredibly valuable in helping me feel comfortable and get established in my company and community. This book is vital for anyone starting their career, in a new job, or moving."

— Rachel Michaelson, MBA, Senior Analyst

"I used to hate networking events, in part because I didn't know how to do them effectively to benefit my business. When I met Beth, I watched her sincere, natural and relaxed way of interacting with people and I learned so much! Then I found out she was writing down all of her secrets in this book and I begged her to finish it as quickly as possible. It is the key to turning new connections into customers and advocates for your business."

— Melissa Tosetti, Founder of The Savvy Life,
   international bestselling author of
   Living The Savvy Life

"Beth has been teaching business people how to effectively network in real world situations for many years and is widely recognized for her passion and proficiency in this often misunderstood skill set. And now she has put her expertise into a concise, easy to understand instruction manual that you can use to increase your business development effectiveness immediately. In Networking on Purpose, Beth shows you how to network without selling and build the kind of relationships that lead to business."

— Dale Bierce, Sandler Training

"A chamber of commerce should be at the business front in setting the standards in their community with quality networking. It's appropriate that this book and the simple but powerful strategy within it, comes from a very experienced and amazing chamber of commerce executive. If you have joined a chamber of commerce and wonder just what do I do next, 'Networking on Purpose' is your practical, easy-to-use guide for making the most of the networking opportunities in your organization and community. This is a must read for chambers, members and businesses! Beth is doing awesome and mighty things in her community. With this plan, you can do the same."

— Lisa Farquharson, President/CEO, The Dalles
Chamber of Commerce

"Women are natural relationship-builders, but we still need a strategic plan. The Five-Part Success Plan is simple enough to remember and powerful enough to help you build the network you need. I had to learn much of this the hard way, over time. You have the opportunity to significantly shorten your learning curve."

— Lucia Robeson, Banking Business Relationship
Manager

"Research has shown that one of the top reasons businesses join a chamber is for business exposure and connections. Finally, someone has come up with a simple but powerful strategy to help businesses in these areas. Beth is now emerging as a leader in the chamber industry with this book. All members of the chamber's staff should read this book, learn, apply and teach these principles to make their business community even stronger."

— Steve Snyder, Vice President, Western Association of
Chamber Executives (WACE)

Networking on Purpose

A Five-Part Success Plan to Build a Powerful and Profitable Business Network

Beth Bridges

TheNetworkingMotivator.com

Networking on Purpose: A Five-Part Success Plan to Build a Powerful and Profitable Business Network
by Beth Bridges

Copyright © 2013 Elizabeth Bridges

The Networking Motivator ™ is a trademark of Beth Bridges
The Five-Part Networking Success Plan ™ is a trademark of Beth Bridges

ISBN: 978-0-9897553-0-6
First Edition 2013
Published by iBridge Enterprises
Fresno, California
www.TheNetworkingMotivator.com

Cover design by Kimb Manson Graphic Design,
www.senjula.com

Photography by Everett Photography,
www.EverettPhotography.com

Interior design by Susan Daffron,
www.SusanDaffron.com

Logo design by Damon Thomas,
www.pixel-polygon.com

Contents

Foreword

by Bob Burg,
co-author of *The Go-Giver* and
author of *Endless Referrals*

Networking: it's a term that, while used as part of common business vernacular since the mid-1970s and utilized in one way or another perhaps since humankind began, is actually understood by relatively few people, and is effectively utilized by far fewer. Just say the very word and visions of the stereotypical networking sales guy pop into peoples' minds, along with such trite phrases as "have your people call my people" and "let's do lunch." Not to mention the flurry of business cards being exchanged between parties, each grabbing for air space in order to promote his or her business (which may sound to most readers like the "waa-waa-waa" of the *Peanuts®* cartoon fame).

And then, every so often, a master comes along to show us the way—the correct way—the effective way. In this case, her name is Beth Bridges. I've known Beth for several years, beginning on social media and as a commenter on my blog posts, and she quickly became a valued friend.

One thing that is very noticeable in any exchange I've had with Beth is that she really knows her topic, and that topic is networking.

As the Membership Director and Chief Networking Officer of a large California Chamber of Commerce, it was her job to understand networking and be able to effectively teach it to others. This she does with flying colors. It was also interesting to me that when I was scheduled to speak at an event in Fresno, California—the next town over—I asked my client if she knew of Beth, and the answer was immediate, affirmative, and provided with a great deal of respect. When I asked two different Fresno media personalities (who were interviewing me about my upcoming event) if they knew Beth, their responses were the same as my client's. Actually, when asking anyone about Beth...same response.

She has earned the responses of know, like (actually, more like love), and trust from others, which are signs that she is a person who truly understands networking.

The book's very title provides the premise: it's not a matter of just going out there willy-nilly into the business community. It's not simply doing some of the correct things here and there. It's Networking *on* Purpose and *with* a purpose: to bring exceptional value to the lives and businesses of many people, and create a context for the same to happen for you and your business. And all parties benefit to a huge degree along the way, as a result.

Through her Five-Part Networking Success Plan™, you'll learn all the skills you need to become a master networker.

This book is short, it's easy-to-read, and it is packed with so many nuggets of golden wisdom that you'll be able to use it as your ongoing guide for successful networking for as long as you're in business. My only other suggestion is to buy a copy for any young person you know who will one day need this information. Actually, it's never too early for them to learn this information, because it's not just a matter of being successful in business, but one of being successful in...life!

Near the end of the book, in taking her curtain call, Beth writes:

"My goal was to give you as much value as possible in as compact a book as possible."

This she did, and she did it outstandingly well!

Bob Burg

burg.com

Introduction

You want more from your business so you can have more time with your family and all the other things you love in your life. As our society becomes increasingly complex, we're expected to do more with every minute of the day. How can we possibly do this? Through networking.

Your network is leverage. It gives you access to resources. It saves you time in finding solutions. It provides you with knowledge and ideas. A network helps you build a foundation for future success.

When I started working in association management twenty years ago, I didn't have a plan; I had no strategy. I just knew what I liked to do and what seemed to work. Ten years ago, I took a position as the membership director of a large west-coast chamber of commerce. There was no marketing or advertising budget to build up membership. The only tool

I had was networking. I couldn't "wing it" any more. I needed to know exactly what to do so I could get more out of my efforts.

I became an active and intense networker. In the last ten years, I've been to over 2,200 networking events, from small luncheons to massive conferences. I've become very good at meeting new people, sharing value with them, and getting great benefit in return for myself, for the chamber, and for thousands of small business owners, employees, and job seekers whom I've met along the way.

There was clearly a simple plan and fundamental actions that I was taking to build this network. I began searching for the words to describe exactly what I was doing. I wanted to know how to explain, share, and teach what I was doing so that others could build a successful networking strategy, too.

I studied my own actions and those of successful networkers from around the world. I discovered that there is a very simple networking plan and a clear purpose that anyone can learn and apply. Along the way, I realized that what I was doing is more than networking; it's Networking on Purpose.

Networking on Purpose is your blueprint for building a powerful and profitable business network. You'll instantly learn strategies and techniques that took me years to develop. I'll reveal the underlying purpose of networking and the reason for everything you'll do. You'll get a definition of networking that clarifies what it is and that works for in-person and on-line networking. I'll teach you the simple actions that make up the Five-Part Networking Success Plan™.

Networking on Purpose means that instead of wondering what to do, you'll always know what's next. Instead of feeling confused, you'll be strong and confident. Instead of following others, you'll become a leader. Instead of wasting time, you'll make every minute count.

It's time for you to begin networking on purpose.

Chapter 1

Networking on Purpose

*"Efforts and courage are not enough
without purpose and direction."*

— John F. Kennedy

Why do you want to network? What do you want it to do for you? Do you want to get a new job? Find new sources of clients? Promote your company's reputation? Anything you can imagine that has a physical outcome is only the *result* of networking.

The *purpose* of networking is to put yourself in a position to give and receive value.

This can be a physical position: being in the right place at the right time with the right people. It's also a mental position: being at the "top of mind" when other people need something. When you learn the Five-Part Networking Success Plan™, you'll see that each part is designed to move you into those physical and mental places.

> *The purpose of networking is to put yourself in a position to give and receive value.*

You'll be a successful networker when you know the purpose of networking and combine it with action. Most people network without a strategy. If you have a plan for your networking efforts, you'll always know which direction to go instead of randomly moving around. Instead of wondering if you're doing the right things, you'll always know what to do. Instead of hoping for results, you'll know exactly how networking works and how to get the results you want.

Networking on Purpose will make it easier for you to find and connect to people who can help you. It will give you confidence in knowing that no effort is wasted. It'll produce benefits for you and for the people around you.

Networking on Purpose means that you know what to do, when to do it, and what to do next. When you know your purpose, you can make relentless progress toward any goal.

What Is Networking?

"All things being equal, people will do business with, and refer business to, those people they know, like, and trust."

— Bob Burg

It's the most equal opportunity business tool in the world. You don't have to be a genius. Or rich. Or beautiful. Networking is simple; learn the everyday actions that you need to take. Networking is cheap; it doesn't cost thousands of dollars to leverage it for your business. Networking is for everyone; success doesn't depend on having a certain personality style.

It's available for all, but misunderstood by many. Schmoozing, socializing, meet-and-greet, sucking up, brown-nosing, sweet-talking, politics, pandering...I've heard all these words, usually used after these words: "Networking? Isn't it just..."

If you've thought the same thing, then you haven't seen networking done right. Or you've been the target of sales pitches and insincere flattery in the guise of networking. That's not networking. It's absolutely not networking on purpose.

> ***Networking on purpose is the ongoing process of building long-term, mutually beneficial relationships through the sharing of ideas, information, resources, and experiences.***

Networking on Purpose is the ongoing process of building long-term, mutually beneficial relationships through the sharing of ideas, information, resources, and experiences.

Your *network* is made of people who feel connected to you. They are willing to share ideas, information, resources, and experiences with you. They want to do business with you and they are the people with whom you want to do business.

It's a *process*. You can't network once and be done. When you network on purpose, there's a clear series of actions to move you forward and build your network. It's *ongoing* for the best results. I see people actively network only long enough to get the result they want and then they stop—until they need something again. Then it's desperate networking time again.

Networking works best with *long-term relationships*. Society functions because of our ties to our family, our community, and common humanity. The biggest favors, the most dependable resources, and the best opportunities come through people we've known over time. Helpful short-term interactions can take place. We can go to an event where we can get a great insight or suggestion from someone we just met. But the longer you work on building a relationship, the bigger and better the benefits to both of you.

Mutually beneficial means that both sides get something out of their interaction and out of the relationship. It won't be an equal exchange of objective value. This isn't about a sales transaction where everyone agrees on what is to be paid and what is to be delivered. It's about investing in the future through other people.

Finally, you interact with other people by *sharing ideas, information, resources, and experiences.* Ideas are your creative contributions based on your knowledge and experiences. Information comes from other sources. Resources are tangible items or information that result in a measurable benefit to a person or business.

In business, we tend to focus on sharing ideas, information, and resources. In friendships, it's all about the experiences. How did you make friends as a kid? You spent time together doing "stuff." Whether it's riding bikes, going to the football game with your high school buddies, or hanging out at happy hour with co-workers, all of these are experiences we've shared with other people.

To me, networking *is* about making friends with people. Everything you do in networking is appropriate to building friendships. And there is very little you would do with your friend that doesn't work to strengthen your network. If you want stronger business relationships, share experiences with people. If you're not comfortable with this and you prefer to separate your friends and business contacts, feel free to do that. You don't have to make everyone your friend, but every relationship in your network should be friendly.

> *Networking is investing in the future through other people.*

Finally, here is what networking is not.

Networking is not selling.

We like to buy, but we hate being sold to. And yet the bitterest complaint I hear about networking is that people get sales-pitched at networking events or at a coffee meeting that was supposed to be an opportunity to get to know each other.

We all feel the pressure to get our product or our service out there. To prospect and to find potential buyers. To close the deal. Selling is the most important part of your business. If nothing is sold, there is no business. Selling is extremely important. It is a different activity with its own strategies, skills, and appropriate time and place.

The Five-Part Networking Success Plan™

> *"Simplicity is the ultimate sophistication."*
>
> — Leonardo da Vinci

Want to have a little "business geek" fun? Ask your friends to explain networking in less than a minute or in fewer than fifty words. People end up describing the activities they get involved in or telling you networking stories. They know it's simple, but they can't quite put their finger on the exact terms. Ten years ago, *I* would not have been able to tell you what I was doing in so few words. Developing the Five-Part Networking Success Plan™ was in part an attempt to answer my own question: "What am I doing and how can I share it as simply as possible?"

Now I know the purpose, how it works, and what to always do next. There are only five parts and they are simple, straightforward actions. If you've been networking at random, it's time to put the pieces together. Apply the five parts to your daily routine and you'll be networking on purpose.

The five parts are:

- Believe In _____
- Go Places
- Meet People
- Stay Connected
- Give Value

That's it. Five parts, ten words. If you memorize this, you'll know more about networking and how it works than most people in business today.

> *Apply the Five-Part Success Plan to your daily routine and you'll be networking on purpose.*

It's a simple and flexible plan. You can use it as a general outline. You

16

can use it to create a detailed guide for your daily actions. If you're completely new to networking, it'll give you a solid framework to start networking on purpose. If you've been frustrated with networking in the past, it'll explain what wasn't working for you and how to get back on purpose. If you're an experienced networker, you can fine tune your own approach and share this resource with your friends who are still learning.

Believe In _____

Yourself, first and foremost. Know that you have the ability to network regardless of your experience, your personality style, or your job situation. Believe in the process of networking on purpose. Believe that it's the most powerful personal branding and business development tool that you have. When you understand how to network on purpose, you'll have confidence in yourself and in the process.

Go Places

You transform yourself physically and mentally when you go places designed for networking. Before you go anywhere, you put your mind in a positive place. Arriving at an event tells people that you're going to be valuable to them. When you're networking on purpose, every destination matters. Your body is positioned to interact and your mind is open to possibilities.

Meet People

The secret to easily meeting new people is to network with like-minded people. Not people who are the same as you, but those who are networking on purpose (whether they know it or not). Your network needs to grow and expand to include these people. The more of them you know, the more opportunities you'll have to give and receive value.

Stay Connected

People want to feel that they belong and that they matter. We all want to be connected to other people in a meaningful way. When you make the effort to stay connected with someone, you show them that they are important to you and that they matter. There is an ongoing opportunity to give them value and create a relationship. Staying connected gives them the opportunity to get to know you, trust you, and like you.

Give Value

Everything else in the networking success plan is designed to put you in a position to give value—not only to give value, but to give it first. By giving value, you build up a reserve of goodwill. By giving value, you inspire other people to give, creating a cascade of helpful and positive behavior. By giving value, you're networking on purpose and you'll receive value in return.

The Five-Part Networking Success Plan™ is simple. It includes everything that you need to do and leaves out everything that isn't networking. Want to be sure you're networking on purpose? Check to see if what you're doing fits into one of the five parts.

For example, if you hand out a business card along with your elevator pitch, is that networking? Where does it fit in the five parts? Does it help you meet people? If they don't get to say anything besides "hello," there's not much of a connection. Does it give value? Most of us don't count an unsolicited sales pitch as having value. If you're ever in doubt about what you're doing, look at the five parts.

- *Believe in* ____ explains *why* you network.

- *Go places* describes *where* you need to be.

- *Meet people* tells you *who* to meet and how to meet them.

- *Staying connected* is *how* you maintain relationships.

- Give value is *what* you do to build powerful
  connections.

In the next five chapters, I'll give you dozens of
ways to apply each of these parts so you can begin
building your own profitable and powerful network.

Chapter 2

Believe In _____

"Do the thing and have the power."

— Ralph Waldo Emerson

I believe that networking makes my personal and business life easier and makes me more effective. I believe that a strong network can help solve any problem I have. I believe that it is the most important and valuable business development strategy anyone can have, whether you are a one-person business, an independent contractor, or a corporate CEO. I believe in networking on purpose.

You don't have to believe any of this.

Not at first. All you really need to believe in right now is your ability to take action. Believe in your own willingness to act. And then do something. The universe rewards action.

The physical world doesn't depend on belief. Things work whether you believe it or not. It doesn't matter if you don't believe that hitting your thumb with a hammer will hurt. It will. If you start doing the simple parts of networking, you will start networking on purpose, whether or not you believe it works.

If you don't believe *and* you don't take action, then you'll never be successful. There are millions of unsuccessful people out there waiting until they "know" something will work before they try it. Or they are waiting for the power, or the motivation, or the inspiration to come. Or for the fear to go away. They are going to be waiting for a long time. The advantage goes to those who take action.

You have to put something out before you get anything back. You wouldn't buy a tomato seedling, plant it in the ground, and then tell it, "You'll get water as soon as I get tomatoes!" Of course not. You know that the plant has to go into the ground and be watered and nurtured first.

Believe in your ability to take action.

Emerson didn't say, "Wait until you have power and then do something." Start building your network even if you're not certain it will work. Take the right actions and you'll get results that will make a difference in your business and life. Positive results will encourage and motivate you to do more. And as you start seeing results, your belief will build.

What Not to Believe

"I want to believe."

— Fox Mulder

You may want to believe in the power of networking. If you haven't started or if you feel stuck, check to see if you have negative beliefs that are stopping you. There are three common misconceptions:

- "I have to get over my fear before I start."
- "Only extroverts are good at networking."
- "I will get sales at networking events."

"I have to get over my fear before I start."

False. This is not about fear. Except for near-collisions on the freeway, few things in our modern life cause us genuine, heart-pounding fear. This is about being in an uncomfortable or unfamiliar situation that we don't enjoy. Unless you have a phobia, what you feel is discomfort and strangeness. There are two ways to get over this discomfort.

You can plunge in all at once. Schedule a few weeks of as many networking events and activities as you can find. It's not a pace you'll keep up for long, but you'll get comfortable with the feeling very quickly.

Then there's the get-warmed-up-first approach. It's like getting into a cold swimming pool—you start with your toes and wait for them to get comfortable. Start with a familiar group and work toward gradually more challenging situations. Use the buddy system and go to an event with a friend. Eventually work your way up to events where you don't know anyone.

Both methods work as long as you keep moving forward. If you're not feeling more comfortable at each event, you're taking too long in between them. Everyone can become more confident by taking consistent action. There's only one person who gets left out of the fun: the one who waits for the water to get warm. You don't become more confident by sitting around and wishing for it to happen. Confidence and comfort are built by taking action and experiencing a series of small successes.

"Only extroverts are good at networking."

False. Extroverts are energized by interaction with other people. They get their energy from talking with people and being around others. They are seen as sociable, outgoing, and talkative. This is the stereotype of a good networker. Networking on purpose involves a great deal more than talking to people.

Introverts get energy from their inner thoughts and from quiet, reflective activities on their own or with a few good friends. They are seen as being thoughtful and good listeners. They can be mislabeled as shy.

If networking were a talent, it might be an advantage to be an extrovert. Instead, networking is a skill that can be learned by everyone. Extroverts do have strengths, but they also have weaknesses. Introverts have disadvantages in some situations, but they have strengths that are un-

> *Networking is a skill that can be learned by everyone.*

der-used and under-appreciated. If you're an introvert, give yourself permission to acknowledge that networking is hard work—it is for everyone. Don't let the feeling of being tired or drained fool you into thinking you failed. Only the most extreme extroverts are ready to go to another party after a long mixer or trade show.

Most people are ambiverts; they act extroverted or introverted, depending on the situation. Only a small portion of the population is always extroverted or always introverted. I have a friend who owned a retail store. Inside the store, she was the life of the party. People would come to her shop just to hang out with her.

I invited her to networking events and she kept turning me down. She finally told me that she was an introvert. I almost didn't believe it, but she said she just didn't feel comfortable at outside networking events. Would you label my friend as introverted or extroverted? She had her comfort zone and within it, she was an extrovert.

The people at networking events who are talking, laughing and mingling might be ambiverts, too, but that event has become part of their comfort zone. Ambiverts and introverts can easily be comfortable in more places by learning to network on purpose and expanding their comfort zones.

"I will get sales at networking events."

False. No one wants to be on the receiving end of a sales pitch at a networking event. In behavioral economics there are social norms and market norms. Social norms are situations where there is an exchange of favors between friends and acquaintances. It is an interaction that's not based on a dollar value. You don't pay your mother-in-law for cooking a fabulous dinner at Thanksgiving. You don't do your friend a favor and then ask him or her to pay for your time.

Market norms are situations where we do expect to pay for something. At the store there's a price tag on the bread. We call a tow truck and we pay now or go nowhere. It's awkward when these two norms get mixed up. Imagine if your mother-in-law asked everyone at the dinner to pay for their meal. Or if you asked the tow-truck driver to get you to the garage as a favor. That's why the sales pitch feels so unpleasant at a networking event. It's out of place where people are expecting to renew contacts, meet new people, and build their social connections...not buy things.

Relax. The sales will come. Networking is not selling, but it *leads* to more sales. When you put yourself in a position to give and receive value, you will get more sales. Networking on purpose gives you visibility, exposure, stronger relationships, and more access to resources. Networking on purpose keeps you focused on the social norms that will build your reputation and your business.

How to Find Your Motivation

"People often say that motivation doesn't last. Well, neither does bathing; that's why we recommend it daily."

— Zig Ziglar

If you don't have a built-in belief in the value of networking on purpose, what's going to get you started? Whatever you're passionate about. It's whatever you love that gets you up each morning and keeps you going. You'll need it to overcome the obstacles that come your way.

If it weren't for problems, I could accomplish everything I wanted. I'd just get up, do the things I needed to do, and *viola!* one day my goal would be achieved. Of course, the real world doesn't work that way. No path to success is smooth; otherwise everyone would be successful. Life throws hurdles in our way. The daily grind gets us down. We have to continually motivate ourselves. Motivation, fueled by your positive beliefs, will get you over the inevitable difficulties.

What if you had a motivation so powerful and inspiring that no obstacle could stop you? What could you accomplish then? We *think* the incentive is our material goal. But that isn't the deeper reason why we get up and work hard every day.

Steve Siebold, author of *177 Mental Toughness Secrets of the World Class* says that champions are driven by emotional motivators, not logical reasons or benefits. We're accustomed to thinking the benefits of our actions are enough motivation. But this is logic-based. Your reason—your motivation—has to be emotion-based.

"I want to _____, so that (or *to have*) _____ because _____."

Give yourself the most powerful result and dig deeply into your emotions. Start with a benefit that appeals to you and put it in the first blank. For example, *get more clients*. Your sentence now reads, "I want to get more clients, to have ..." What? What is the purpose of having more clients? To have more money, experience more stability, grow the business?

Because why? What does the money do for you? It helps you retire early. Now your statement is "I want to get more clients to have more money, because I want to retire early." Are you finished? Is that a strong enough motivating statement? Is there enough emotion tied to it? If the *because* doesn't choke you up a little, this motivating statement will not work.

If the *because* is not emotionally compelling, keep going. Repeat the *so that/to have* and *because* statements until you have an emotional statement. "I want to get more clients to make more money, because I want to retire early, so I can travel the country with my with my husband, because he's never traveled and because I love him and want him to experience the wonders of the world by my side."

Which part of that statement would make you get up early every Tuesday for your leads club meeting? More clients, or traveling the country with your spouse?

Here's another example:

"I want to expand my contacts to create a safety net because my children ask me if I could lose my job and I want them to feel proud and confident that Mommy has lots of friends who would help her find a better job really fast." If that doesn't touch your heart, then what would?

The final statement must be a positive, love-based statement. Siebold emphasizes that great people evolve from fear-based to love-based motivation. If your last *because* is fear-based, keep going until the last statement is based on love for someone or something. Fear saps your strength. Move toward something positive, not away from something negative. Your *why* must be positively motivating to help you achieve great results and break through obstacles.

Write down your motivating statement, post it, and review it when you feel tired or discouraged. This love-filled, emotional statement will give you the strength to keep networking on purpose.

The Benefits of Networking

"Good fortune is what happens when opportunity meets with planning."

— Thomas Edison

There's a difference between having goals for your networking efforts and networking on purpose to acquire benefits. Goals are specific outcomes. They can be easily described and tracked. Meeting a particular person, going to a certain event, and making X contacts with your existing network are goals.

The benefits of networking are bigger than the specific goals you will achieve. Goals are set, achieved, and then you move on to the next one. Benefits have a value that you build up. Every time you achieve or receive something of worth, you become more valuable to other people. What do you want to receive? What is it that you value and what benefits can networking give you?

> *Every time you achieve or receive something of worth, you become more valuable to other people.*

Information

There's more to know about running a business than any one person can learn in a lifetime. Other people have expertise in areas you don't. They've learned from experiences you haven't had. They know about unadvertised job openings, who the key contacts are, and when new businesses are about to open. A powerful network shares their information and shortens our learning curve.

Ideas

While Einstein's theories were developed inside his head, almost everyone else's great ideas come from working with other people. Your ideas help you get more creative in building your business. They also inspire others and give them leverage for developing their own great ideas.

Resources

In business management, resources include capital (i.e. money), equipment, and human resources. No small business ever has enough money to do all the things they want to do, but a strong network will stretch every dollar. Trade-outs, borrowing, and bartering take place in an environment of trust. Referrals are resources that come from satisfied customers and active connections. A network is the best way to find the right people to grow your business.

Marketing

"Marketing is everything," says Robert Mano, author of *Thinking Beyond the Obvious*. A business without marketing or without an awareness of what marketing is and how to leverage it is out of business. Networking is one of your marketing tools. If you don't have a budget for advertising, PR, or direct-marketing campaigns, then networking, prospecting, and selling are your no- and low-cost options. Networking is a powerful marketing channel for promoting your image and developing your brand.

Reputation

Your reputation is worth money in the form of referrals, resources, and sales that you make because of it. While eBay has a buyer/seller rating, there isn't a universal personal quality-rating service. Until there is one, the only way that people know they can trust you is through their experience with you or through conversations with people in your network.

Social Capital

You can build social capital by helping other people and giving them value. People will remember that you gave value to them without asking for payment in return. Their memory is a resource for return favors that you can draw upon. You make deposits into your social capital "account" that you can pull from later. The metaphor isn't perfect, though. Unlike a CD or savings account, social capital doesn't earn interest. Instead, it can leach away with time, so you need to keep making deposits.

Referrals

Referrals are the payout for developing your reputation, seeking out information, and sharing ideas. Referrals give a high return on investment because you don't have to pay for advertising or direct mail. You are much more likely to make the sale with someone who was referred to you. And a referred client is much more likely to give you the benefit of the doubt if mistakes are made.

Sales

Seek to make sales as a *result* of networking, not *while* networking. Business people all have a product, service, or a cause to sell. If you're networking at business events, everyone is aware of this. Look for opportunities to solve people's problems, whether your business is the solution or not.

When you share ideas and information, you get access to more resources. By building on your reputation, you'll get more referrals. When you help other people, you build your social capital. And referrals are among the most cost-effective ways of getting new customers. Your sales go up and your cost of acquiring new customers goes down.

> *Seek to make sales as a result of networking, not while networking.*

35

Believe In _____ Recap

*"What the mind of man can conceive
and believe, it can achieve."*

— Napoleon Hill

You don't have to believe at first. You just have to believe enough to be willing to try. Believe in your ability to take action. Do the work and you'll find out that it *will* work for you.

Know what not to believe. Some common myths stop many people from taking any action. The important thing to remember is that:

- You do not have to get rid of fears or discomfort before starting to network.
- Extroverts are not automatically better at networking than introverts.
- Networking is not the place or time to be selling.

Motivation is what propels us to action. We are not motivated by our goals, but by strong emotional needs. The most effective drivers are the positive, love-based feelings for our self, our family, and our future. Finding this core motivation is how we fuel the belief that gets us going.

I believe that networking on purpose will make your personal and business life better. There are short-term goals to be achieved along the way, using the Five-Part Networking Success Plan™. The benefits are long-term, because they add value to you and your network.

The benefits of networking on purpose are:

- Information
- Ideas
- Resources
- Market Exposure
- Positive Reputation
- Referrals
- Social Capital
- Sales

Get more ideas on how to believe in yourself and in the networking process at www.theNetworking-Motivator.com.

What do you believe in ...?

Chapter 3

Go Places

"All you have to do is know where you're going. The answers will come to you of their own accord."

— Earl Nightingale

G oing places is the key to leveraging the next three parts. You meet far more people when you get out of the zone between your house and your cubicle. You can stay connected with people in places where you'll see them. Giving value can be easily accomplished by sharing ideas or information at events or meetings.

New networkers can get stuck on the question of where to go because they don't have a strategy for going places. They get invited to the same luncheon haunted by the rest of the company representatives. Or they get told to go anywhere and just talk to anyone who gets within three feet of them. Or they don't go anywhere because they don't want to go to giant mixers. You will be successful if you go to networking events, which are places you go to be in a position to give and receive value.

A networking event is any activity where two or more people come together on purpose to create, develop, and expand relationships. This includes luncheons, mixers, receptions, association meetings, seminars, trade shows, and one-to-one meetings.

> *A networking event is any activity where two or more people come together to build business relationships.*

Yes, two people getting together for coffee, tea, breakfast, lunch, dinner, or drinks is a networking event. Just one meeting a week with a potential new contact adds up to more than fifty per year. You can build a powerful network without ever setting foot inside a luncheon or mixer. Plan on adding them as you gain experience and get more comfortable with the process, in order to leverage your efforts. Luncheons and mixers can be a valuable use of your time because:

- You can meet a variety of people.

- You have access to a variety of businesses.

- You get outside your usual circle of friends.

- You get to know people when you attend regularly.

- You benefit from the organizer's influence in attracting people.

- You get a great deal of practice at small talk.

Networking opportunities are available everywhere you go. It's important to find the best places that give you the greatest support for networking on purpose.

Find Places to Network

"There are many ways of going forward,
but only one way of standing still."

— Franklin D. Roosevelt

Every month I speak on the Five-Part Networking Success Plan™ to a group of job seekers through a program called *Experience Unlimited*. For several years I surveyed the members of the group to find out what their biggest networking challenge was. To my surprise, it was, by far, that they simply didn't know where to go to network.

You may be in a similar position. Ready to go, ready to start, but not sure where to begin. Or you attend a few regular events and activities, but you want to expand your reach. Either way, there are plenty of ways to find events and organizations once you know where to look.

Ask Around

Check with business people you already know about networking events and organizations that they are a part of. Go to the neighbors in your office complex, introduce yourself, and ask for networking suggestions. You'll get ideas and meet people at the same time.

Local Paper

Check the business section of the local paper for event listings (online and print). Their calendar may not list events until the day of the event, which is not helpful if it's a 7:00 a.m. meeting. Research the group and if you appreciate what they have to offer, work it into your schedule. Most organizations meet at least once a month, so stick with the search to get a full cycle of events in the area.

Business Papers

A business newspaper is a specialty publication that focuses on business events, articles, and information. Check their calendar for a variety of groups and activities. American City Business Journals, Inc. publishes papers in 41 major metropolitan areas in the United States. Look for locally owned papers by searching for your city name and the phrase "business newspaper."

Search Engines

Search for networking organizations or events by using words such as association, service club, chapter, network, trade group, business or trade organization, or professional group. Narrow it down by adding your industry description and city name. A wide range of international associations may have chapters in your city or locale. Wikipedia has a list for the United States that covers everything from the extremely large Alliance of Automobile Manufacturers to the very specialized Cordage Institute; your business specialty or industry surely has representation. Find lists for other countries by searching for "industry trade groups Australia, the U.K., etc.

National Associations

Your online search will turn up a multitude of options. If a local chapter isn't near you, you can always join the national association. The benefits can include training, discounts, and a growing number have online networking and discussion boards. You also have the advanced networking alternative of starting your own local chapter. If you're not an experienced networker when you start this project, you'll be one when you finish.

The Best Places to Start

While you can meet people anywhere, focus on places where you're going to get the best response. Some organizations are designed just to bring business people together. I recommend you start by seeking these organizations and types of events.

Chamber of Commerce

The local chamber of commerce is an association dedicated to the success of their business community. They are usually the most active networking organization in town, offering one or more of these types of events:

- **After-hours mixers** have no agenda and no structure beyond a start and finish time. You're usually on your own to mingle and meet people. Find out if the chamber has an ambassador or greeters program, which is a group of people whose volunteer job is to help newcomers feel welcome. Introduce yourself to one or two of them in advance of the event (by phone or e-mail) so you know at least one person who is well-known and willing to introduce you to people.

- **Lunch-time trainings** combine networking, food, and learning. They may be casual bring-your-own-lunch events, or they may be catered or held at a restaurant. The organizer's main point is to present information on a useful topic. They provide a good opportunity to meet people who are interested in the same subject or are struggling with the same problem.

- **Leads or referral groups** are valuable networking options. A leads club is a networking group that allows only one person per business category. Members are expected to refer business to each other. This can be incredibly effective if you're in a group with people who are networking on purpose. The best way to *receive* referrals? Make sure you're very clear on describing a good referral and *give* plenty of leads to others in the group.

- **Speed networking** came from the great tradition of speed dating, and it turns the *meat market* into a *meet market*. You sit across from one person at a time and have 2 to 15 minutes for introductions and to learn something about the other person. Then a bell rings and you move to meet the next person. By the end of the event, you'll have made contact with everyone there.

- **Toastmasters** is an international organization that helps people develop speaking and leadership skills. While it's not designed to be a networking group, a chamber-sponsored club will attract business people. This puts you in a position to build long-term relationships with like-minded people. You'll enjoy the bonus of developing communication skills that make networking on purpose easier and more effective.

- **Trade shows** are an excellent option for presenting your business to a wider audience. Most chamber trade shows are free or inexpensive to attend. You get the opportunity to network with other attendees and to introduce yourself to a range of businesses.

Conferences

A conference includes networking, seminars, demonstrations, and trade-show exhibits. Once you've registered, you're committed to several days of meeting other people, fine-tuning your knowledge, and being visible on a large scale. Some events require industry credentials, while others don't care what you do as long as you pay the registration fee. Ask if you can pick and choose a la carte from the networking events.

Service Organizations

Elks, Moose, Odd Fellows, Rotarians, Kiwanis, Lions, Exchange. A complete zoo of organizations can be found in even the smallest cities. They'll have a long history and a clear purpose. Very often, they'll be the networking home of the movers and shakers in your area.

Local Independent Groups

You'll find a variety of local or regional groups designed for networking that are independent of any national agency. A good portion of them may be women's organizations, started in the 1980s as women entered the professional workforce.

Join a Team

You used to have the choice of bowling or joining the company softball team. Today you can find adult teams for soccer, kickball, volleyball, and even dodge ball. Check with your local parks and recreation department. Running and cycling aren't team sports, but there *are* clubs for running and riding in groups. Visit your local running-shoe store and the bike shop to find clubs or to connect with other people who are looking for running or riding buddies. Search MeetUp.com and Facebook for team and sports groups, too.

Go Places in No Time (Social Media)

"When you give everyone a voice and give people power, the system usually ends up in a really good place."

— Mark Zuckerberg

Social media sites are the final frontier of places to go for networking. Ignore the critics who say that you can't really network with people you meet online. If both of you are there to be in a position to give and receive value, then you can network together. Be careful. It's tempting to get online, get sucked in, and never get out of the house. I consider these additional benefits of getting involved in social media networking to be worth the risk:

- It can easily be done in very short chunks of time.

- There's no cost to get started.

- It's the fastest-growing media in human history.

- It reaches around the world.

- It is incredibly easy for you to find specific people.

- It's great for introverted networkers.

- You're more visible to more people at once.

Here are the down sides to social media networking. It can be time-consuming; Facebook is designed to get you to spend as much time on it as possible. There is a learning curve. Instead of trying to learn a specific site, work on learning how to get up to speed as quickly as possible. You'll also get hit on, spammed, and sold to online just as you do in the real world. Don't let that keep you from getting involved. You don't stop talking to people (in general) in real life because you don't like what they say. Social media is better because you can block all the game invitations and hide unfriendly posts or nasty comments. It's the digital equivalent of sticking your fingers in your ears, and no one can see you do it. Where do you start?

Facebook

Because everyone is on it.

Facebook claims to have over 800 million active users with 50% of them logging in every day. More users equal more visibility and more potential connections. Finding time to get onto Facebook is usually not a problem; the trick is to spend your time networking on purpose.

LinkedIn

Because it's all business.

It's completely SFW (suitable for work), because there are no photos outside of the profile picture, which LinkedIn monitors. Designed less for entertainment, it's more for making connections and building careers. Instead of highlighting likes, hobbies, and pages, your profile is laid out in resume format. Recruiters are regular participants and they search profiles for keywords to find the right person for their job openings.

Industry-Specific Sites

Because you need to be with your peers.

You need to go places—in person and online—where you'll find the people who make the decisions in your industry. Search for a discussion board, Facebook page, LinkedIn group or other forum for your job description or industry.

It is important that you:

- Plan your social media sites as strategically as you would any physical real-world event.

- Add your chosen social media sites to your go-to list.

- Spend your time online on purpose to maximize your networking benefits.

Networking is easier and more effective not just because of social media sites; technology in general is making a difference. Skype, texting, QR codes, and tablet computing make communicating easier, any time and anywhere, with almost anyone. While the technology will constantly change—people under 25 now send text messages, not email—the need to be visible and to connect with other people will not change.

The Google+ Hangout is a fantastic tool for using technology to connect with a small group. I use it to meet with other authors to share strategies, ideas, and encouragement. Frank Kenny, author of *The 7 Secrets Laws of Society: Social Media Essentials and Strategies for Small Businesses and Associations*, provides great value to his potential clients (chamber executives) with a guest speaker and informative discussion every week via Google

> *Technology changes, but the need to connect with other people does not.*

Hangouts. It was easy for him to find and invite that specific group because Frank had already created a list of chamber executives on Facebook.

Free vs. Paid Networking

"There's no such thing as a free lunch."

— Milton Friedman

Everyone loves something that is free. No-cost networking events are high on my list. You get to meet a wide variety of people, the venue is usually attractive, and food is almost always available. It's not just networking; it's a free dinner. If you're just getting started with networking and building your social skills, free events are a good way to start.

Practice your small talk, get comfortable going to groups, and explore the business-networking scene in your city without taking any financial risk. Look for open houses, grand openings, chamber mixers, meet-up networking groups, and social after-hours events put on by local association chapters and other organizations.

The potential down side of a free event is that it may be open to anyone and everyone. The people attending might be there for serious networking or they might be there for the food. They could be highly focused decision-makers or they might not believe in investing anything in networking. If they aren't willing to invest in themselves, they might not be willing to invest in you and a future relationship with you.

Once you have a little experience under your belt, paid networking events will provide a better return on your investment. Association meetings, luncheons, and chamber of commerce and service club memberships all come with a price, but are worth more than the cost.

Meet people who are willing to invest in themselves.

You'll meet other people who are willing to invest in themselves. You'll also be able to focus on more specific industries. You'll find more people who are involved in larger companies and who are more likely to be decision makers within those companies. Paid events filter out the lookie-loos. People who pay $20 for a rubber chicken lunch aren't there for the food; they are there to network on purpose. That purpose could include meeting someone like you.

I've already said that I favor chambers of commerce as one of the best places to invest your networking dollars. They have a variety of networking events. They've already attracted relationship-oriented business people and the cost of events is covered in part or in full by your membership dues. They also have a person on staff whose success depends on *you* finding success in your networking experience with the chamber. This could be the membership director, membership relations manager, or the vice president of membership. Imagine having a full-time staff person dedicated to creating great networking events and helping you make more connections. Make an effort to build a relationship with this person so you can be more successful in your local chamber.

Invest in coffee futures. The more people you buy coffee for, the better your future. Remember: a networking event is any time you get together with at least one person to get to know the person and build your relationship. We'll talk more about meeting people, but going to coffee is a great answer to this question: "I've met someone I want to network with, but what do I do next?" Buying coffee is paid networking with a low cost and high return.

You'll have to invest a greater amount of time and money to meet with large business owners, C-level executives, and other tough-to-reach people. They count on these barriers-to-entry to protect themselves from hundreds of sales pitches. You have to earn the opportunity to meet these VIPs. Local service clubs such as Rotary might be a good place to start making that bigger investment.

At the highest level are organizations such as CEO Space or Vistage. Dues can be thousands of dollars and have strict membership qualifications, but you will be in very exclusive company. With the right preparation, these organizations can be incredibly valuable because of the concentration of people who are willing and able to invest a great deal in the group and themselves.

Go Places Recap

"Only those who will risk going too far can possibly find out how far one can go."

— T. S. Eliot

All of your networking success hinges on the starting point, which is your ability to go places where you can be in a position to give and receive value. There are simple ways to find events and organizations:

- Ask your business friends and neighbors.

- Check the newspaper.
- Find a local business journal.
- Search the Internet.

Focus on organizations and events that are dedicated to helping business people meet each other and gain exposure, including:

- Chamber of commerce events: mixers, lunch-and-learns, leads clubs, and speed networking
- Toastmasters
- Trade shows
- National associations and their local chapters
- Conferences
- Service organizations
- Local independent groups
- Recreational sports teams

Social media provides a great way to save time meeting people and staying connected. I consider going online to be an important part of Go Places. Start with two of the biggest social networks — Facebook and LinkedIn—and then add one or two industry-specific sites.

If you're just starting out, go to free events. You'll save money and you'll still meet plenty of people. When you want to meet more specific people and want to build a network with more serious networkers, be ready to invest in membership and event fees.

Get more ideas on where to go at www.theNetworkingMotivator.com

Where will you go to network on purpose?

Chapter 4

Meet People

"People are strange,
when you're a stranger."

— Jim Morrison

No matter how big your network, you need to meet new people. They'll energize you. They'll expand your comfort zone and your area of influence. They'll bring new ideas, information, and resources to your existing network. They'll also make up for the people who are leaving it. Not because you've neglected them, but because things change. People move, pass away, change industries, lose interest, or have goals that significantly diverge from your own.

It can be difficult to meet new people and find a comfortable way to approach total strangers unless you know the secret to meeting new people through networking on purpose:

Network with like-minded people.

Not people who are the same as you, but people who are like-minded in that they, too, are networking on purpose (whether they're aware of it or not). You want every event you go to, every meeting you have, every introduction you get, to be with people who believe that networking is a long-term investment in their business future.

> *The easiest way to meet people is to network with those who are like-minded.*

Don't waste time trying to get through to people who reject the ideas of giving value and staying connected. Focus on people who value long-term, mutually beneficial relationships. This matters whether you're meeting people at a networking event, online, or through a mutual acquaintance.

How to Meet New People

"We meet aliens every day who have something to give us. They come in the form of people with different opinions."

— William Shatner

A trainer in one of the world's most successful direct-sales organizations has a famous strategy for meeting new people. He'll ask an audience if they want to know his secret. They scream, "Yes!" and he says, "Are you sure? It's tricky and complicated." The audience continues to beg him to reveal the big secret. So he tells them "Okay, here we go...ready?" Big pause. Then he sticks out his hand and says, "Hi."

It can be that easy if you've done the research to find the right event. Occasionally you'll run into someone who really did attend just to see the speaker. Or because the boss made them go. You can hope that they have enough manners and social skills to be gracious when you say hello. If not, and you're using your good manners, don't take anyone else's anti-social behavior personally.

If you've gone to the right place, in a like-minded group that attracts those who are there to network and meet new people, it works perfectly. Do this at the grocery store or the gas station and it can get weird. It's why I disagree in one aspect with the "three-foot rule." Some direct-sales/multi-level-marketing organizations teach their associates to meet, talk to, and pitch everyone who gets within three feet of them. That might be a good sales-prospecting technique, but it's not the spirit of networking on purpose.

James Malinchak, speaker, and one of ABC TV's Secret Millionaires, once traveled to an international conference to meet just one person. It was a huge investment in time and money, but James knew that the value of the potential connection was worth the trip. The man he went to meet couldn't believe someone would travel that far to just shake his hand and say "hello." They ended up having dinner that night and working together later. Worth the investment? To James it was.

You might not be in a position to book a last-minute cross-country flight, but would you be willing to drive across town? Make a day trip to a nearby city? How impressed would *you* be if someone drove that far just to meet you? You'd want to know more about why that person values you so much.

Introduce Yourself by Letter or Email

A well-written letter or email can be a powerful way to meet someone. This can't be a form letter with your product features and benefits. That's a sales letter or direct-marketing piece. Your introduction is a way to break the ice and start a conversation. You need a good reason for wanting to meet the person. Trying to sell something is not networking on purpose.

My friend Alan wrote a letter asking to have lunch with a local philanthropist who made major contributions to a university. You can imagine how many requests this man gets and how many he has to turn down. Alan isn't wealthy, he's not a CEO, and he didn't have a business proposal. What he did was research the man he wanted to meet, found out something positive and interesting that most people wouldn't have bothered to learn, and then posed great questions about that knowledge. Alan made himself interesting and asked for the right thing— the opportunity to learn. Did my friend get that lunch meeting? Yes, he did, and they are still in contact to this day.

Introduce Yourself by Public Announcement

There is a dreaded moment in certain events when each person stands up and introduces him- or herself. If you've researched the group, you'll know it's coming and you'll be prepared. This is one of the few occasions when you will use an elevator speech.

I'm not a fan of saying: "I help people with (insert semi-obscure description), but I'm not going to tell you exactly what I do." Here's an approach I *do* like. When you are asked to introduce yourself, state who you are and what you do, then invite them to learn more.

"I find that it's tough to build a relationship with such a brief introduction. I would like to invite you to coffee—my treat—so I can learn more about you and what you do." They've all had too many experiences when they've met someone for coffee and got a sales pitch. If they're skeptical, apply humor: "I promise that if I try to sell you anything, you can dump your coffee in my lap."

Ask for an Introduction

One of the best ways to meet a specific person is through a mutual friend or acquaintance. An introduction from a trusted connection is as powerful as getting a referral. Your friend is going to do more than give out your name and number. He or she will talk about how you know one another, what he or she likes about you, and the business person you are, because it reflects well on him/her.

For this to work, you need to have earned the trust of the person you ask to make the introduction. This person needs to be trusted by the person you want to meet. If you lack credibility with the introducer, you may get a lukewarm introduction. Or none at all. Either way, you'll have put the introducer in an awkward position. If the person you're asking lacks credibility, then you will suffer by association. How do you make sure you're going to be successful in asking for and getting the introduction? If you've been networking on purpose with the person you're asking, then you'll know you've earned the opportunity to ask. And you'll know if the person you're asking is someone who also networks on purpose. The person will have earned the opportunity to make the introduction.

LinkedIn uses this approach. If you don't have a close enough connection, you can ask intermediaries to pass along your request. You have to have the trust of the first person you ask and hope that he or she has built strong relationships, too. The introduction request does give you a place to include a note.

As with any other introduction request, be polite, appreciative, and let the other person know why you want to connect.

Introduce Yourself on Social Media

If you're not already on at least a couple of social media sites, then you've cut yourself off from a significant resource for meeting new people.

During the growth phase of Facebook, people would connect with anyone. It's a much more cautious place now. When you ask someone to connect on LinkedIn, take an extra minute and customize the personal note. On Facebook you have to send a message separately. Let the person know why you're asking to connect.

Feel free to mix and match elements of these messages.

- Hi, it's Bob from the XYZ company, we met at the XYZ luncheon.

- We have a mutual friend.

- I'm a customer/client of (the company you work for).

- I'm a big fan of (movie/book/TV show) too. Not many of us out here, we should stick together.

- I read your book and really appreciated (the message/the information/how helpful it was). Thanks!

Send the friend or connection request first. Then your message can answer the question: "Who is this person and why did he or she ask me to be a friend?"

Business Cards and the Elevator Pitch

> *"If someone likes you,*
> *they'll buy what you're selling,*
> *whether or not they need it."*
>
> — Gene Simmons

At a traditional chamber event called an Ambassador Rally, staff and volunteers gather to learn and share their best practices in helping to promote their chamber of commerce. The participants are the most active members and the best networkers in a chamber of commerce. Usually.

One year, my Ambassadors and I watched a man make his way to every table in the room to ask for business cards. At first, we thought he was one of the organizers gathering them for a door prize drawing. No, he was putting them in his pocket. We wondered what use those cards would be to him, because he didn't even bother to say hello or ask for our names. We took bets on whether we'd get a "nice to meet you" email or if we'd be on a spammy mailing list. Instead, we got nothing. All that work and he didn't even bother to try to sell us something.

Don't be a business-card collector. No one who is networking on purpose will walk through an event just to collect cards and get email addresses. This is the real-life version of the online practice of "email scraping," which results in all the weird offers you get in your inbox. The flip side of this is being a business card distributor. If you've handed your business card to someone who isn't interested and hasn't asked for your card, you've just delivered junk mail without the mailbox.

If you shove your card at everyone, most people will be polite enough to take it, then throw it away later. Most people. A dentist friend of mine gave her card to a man who looked at it, said "I don't need a dentist," and handed the card back to her. She made a small networking error by handing him a card that he hadn't asked for. But he made a bigger error in etiquette by handing it back to her and assuming that she didn't have any other value to offer him.

My "favorite" business-card blunder is to be handed four or five cards and asked to "give these out to your friends." If I've just met you, I haven't had time to learn if I'm ready to refer my friends. Don't focus on giving out cards; be interested in *getting* them. Not to collect them, but to use them as a tool for following up on a new relationship. Get a card from people you've talked to, made a connection with, and have a reason to stay in contact with. A great initial conversation could be wrapped up with: "Sounds like we have some things in common. Let's have coffee." Or "I'd like to learn more about what you do. When can we get together?" Followed by, "May I have your card?"

Then do what you say you're going to do with their information and nothing else. People don't want to be on your email-newsletter or marketing list because they were within arm's reach of you at a networking event.

Although you don't care about handing out your card, you must have them with you. When you ask for someone's card, they'll almost always ask for yours in return. Even though the best networkers know that most of those cards will gather dust, you'll seem unprepared if you don't have one. The rule of thumb is that if you give your card only when asked, you'll be sure to never hand it out inappropriately.

The elevator pitch is misused almost as much as business cards. There's nothing wrong with having one; you just need to know the right time and place to use it. An elevator pitch is a brief summary of your product, your service, and/or what you do. It's called an elevator pitch because it refers to a budding entrepreneur who steps into an elevator with a venture capitalist. There's only a brief elevator trip during which the entrepreneur can give his pitch, capture the VC's interest, and sell the business, so the entrepreneur has to be succinct in saying what he does and want he wants.

You're not looking for investors or trying to close a deal with anyone. All you want to do is share information about yourself in a way that keeps the conversation going. Plan ahead and prepare a very short self-introduction. You will be asked over and over again "what do you do?" You can't fumble around. And you can't take five minutes to explain it—if you do, you will lose your audience. If you try to fit in the product description, value proposition and call to action in your introduction, the answer will likely be "no." Instead of start-

> *Share information about yourself in a way that keeps the conversation going.*

ing a conversation or beginning a new relationship, you've given unsuccessful sales pitch. You'll have to back up and start fresh to present yourself as a connection and not a salesperson - if they give you the opportunity at all.

The Skill of Mingling

> *"I'm not home right now.*
> *I'm out somewhere having a*
> *wonderful time with glamorous people*
> *at fabulous places."*

> — Answering machine message in
> the film *The Running Man*

Mingling. The meet and greet. Being the life of the party. Isn't this the most important part of networking? You go to a different event every day, say "hellooo dahling" to as many people as possible, and then whoosh out the door. Of course not. It's a myth that you need to be a social butterfly to be successful at networking. So is the idea that everyone at a networking event is a stiff-upper-lip old man in a three-piece suit. Or that if you don't fit in, you're not going to be able to meet anyone. Age, race, and gender don't matter. Just seek out people who are like-minded about networking.

You don't have to be the most popular kid in the room, but networking events will be more rewarding if you practice your social skills. Social skills are called "skills" and not "talents" for a reason. You can develop your skills by learning techniques and then practicing them. Good social skills allow us to interact with other people so everyone gets what they want in an environment that is pleasant and cooperative. We need to be good at working with other people to insure that we're in a position to give and receive value more often. Deliver a positive experience to other people who interact with you and you'll have a positive experience. The basic social skills to develop are:

- Making a good first impression.
- Using great manners.
- Carrying on a conversation.
- Listening to others.

People form an opinion of you within seconds of meeting you. If their initial reaction is bad, it will take a several good interactions in the future to sweeten that first sour note. A good first impression is one that reveals your positive personal identity;

you want it to be the most accurate version of your best self.

Be aware of your facial expression and body language. I tend to scrunch my eyebrows when I'm listening intently. What expression is on your face when you're nervous? You might feel silly the first

A good first impression is one that reveals your positive personal identity.

few times you walk into a room with a smile on your face, but it will be attractive. A genuine smile engages the muscles around the eyes, so you can't fake it. Think of something funny if you need a push for your happy face.

Do you cross your arms? To you it's a comfortable place to rest your hands, but it could also appear that you don't want to talk. Are you standing at an open angle with the person you're talking to? That invites others to approach and join your conversation. I once saw a group of three arrive together to a mixer. They spent half an hour in a tight cluster, talking to each other. Their body language didn't invite anyone into their group, and they didn't separate to talk to anyone else. Finally, they left the event (together) after complaining to me that the event was too cliquish.

You are judged by your handshake. A strong handshake conveys strength, genuine warmth, and trustworthiness.

Aim the webbing between your thumb and first finger to meet that of the other person. This prevents the "finger squeeze" or the "royal highness" handshake. Your handshake is firm enough if your palm and fingers are contacting the other person's hand all around. It's too firm if you can feel the bones in the person's hand pushing together, or if he or she stops smiling. If you are a woman, I guarantee you can squeeze harder than you do now. How do you know your handshake is good? Ask a trusted friend to give you honest feedback.

Where do you look when you're talking to someone? It's hard to stay focused at a large networking event—there's so much going on and there are so many people walking around—and one of them may be just the person you want to meet. Don't let your eyes tell your new acquaintance he or she isn't relevant; the person you're talking to right now is the most important one in the room.

People want to be around attractive people. This doesn't mean you have to be gorgeous. A confident, friendly attitude and appropriate attire make everyone attractive. But what is "appropriate?" If it's your first time with a new group, call the host or hostess to ask how people usually dress. No matter what you wear, there are a few firm rules to always remember. Ladies should leave deep cleavage a mystery. Gentlemen should never wear a tie with a short-sleeved shirt. Make sure everything is ironed. The easiest way to spruce up any look is to polish your shoes.

Take a video to see how you look to other people. Yes, this could be a horrifying process. We are all hard on ourselves when we see our funny little expressions or mannerisms, but don't worry; they

The person you're talking to right now is the most important one in the room.

only look funny to you. Focus on what may look unfriendly or off-putting. You can also recruit a trusted friend to evaluate your appearance and handshake. You're not looking for perfection; you just want to be the most approachable and friendly-looking version of yourself.

Etiquette isn't about which fork to use with which course (you start on the outside and work your way in). It's about how your behavior makes other people feel when they are around you. It's also about how you help yourself feel comfortable and appropriate in different situations. Studying etiquette will help you develop important skills such as making good introductions, handling other people's not-so-appropriate behavior, and conducting yourself in a way that reflects well on you. When you know how to make other people feel comfortable, you will feel comfortable. Good manners make you look professional and classy in any situation. As my friend Dallas Teague Snider, author of *Professionally Polished: Business Etiquette Savvy for Today's Competitive Market* likes to say, "You don't have to have money to have class."

You'll be perceived as a much more sociable person if you are able to properly introduce two people. It can be awkward when someone new joins a conversation and other people have to figure out who they are. Be a leader by making everyone feel more comfortable with a great introduction. The additional benefit is that it is much more likely that names will be remembered when there is a clear introduction.

You know how you can always think of the snappy comeback about five minutes too late? Then you practice the conversation in your head over and over—the way you *wanted* it to be. Take that negative habit and turn it into a positive one. You can always find a better way to explain what you do, how you help people, or answer a question about your interests. Rehearse conversations in your head and ask yourself: "What will I say if someone asked this or this?"

Even though you've been talking all your life, you can still work on developing your ability to communicate better with other people. There is nothing wrong with planning what you are going to say ahead of time. You are going to be asked the same questions over and over again; planning ahead allows you to craft the message and the impression you make. Rosalie Maggio, author of *The Art of Talking to Anyone,* includes in her book a huge list of "if they say, you say..." ideas for any occasion.

The final secret to being a great conversationalist is to be a great *listener*. It means keeping your mouth *and* your mind quiet. It doesn't mean holding your tongue long enough for the other person to finish so you can say something clever or interesting. Dale Carnegie taught that to be *interesting*, you must first be *interested*. To be heard, you first have to hear about other people's needs and points of view.

Make Small Talk Significant

*"You never really learn much from
hearing yourself talk."*

— George Clooney

Blah, blah, blah. Feel like everyone is talking but nothing is being said? Don't engage in pointless chit-chat at networking events. Every word that comes out of your mouth should have a purpose. Your first conversation sets the tone for the future relationship. Business topics can lead to referrals, resources, and a growing network. Personal stories can lead to deeper connections.

Do it right and you'll engage more people, build relationships more quickly, and find more ways to give value. Do it wrong and you'll engage in an endless parade of droning conversations that will bore you and others. The right way to converse begins with understanding why we engage in small talk: it gives us time to form or make an impression. We discover common interests. We get the chance to decide whether or not we want to know more about the other person or if we could do business together. It's a way to get comfortable before we move on to sharing our more valuable resources.

78

If networking were all about selling, the alternative to small talk would be to go straight to the close. Imagine going to a networking event, walking up to each person and asking him or her, "Do you want to buy my product?" That's your alternative to engaging in social conversation—"cold-calling" in person. Bad cold-callers try to sell us something without ever asking if it's what we want. Small talk is an opportunity for both people to first learn what the other person wants before there's any talk of products or services.

If you need time to get warmed up, start out talking about traffic or the weather. Be careful; it's too easy to spend twenty minutes on mutual complaining. Most conversations in a business setting start the same way. You each give your name and then one of you says, "What do you do?" It's astonishing how many people seem caught off guard by this question. Expect it and plan your answer ahead of time.

The other person wants to hear something he or she can work with, not a presentation on all your features and benefits. Or a blow-by-blow account of your day. If you're a rocket scientist, don't explain space flight. Just say that you're a rocket scientist. The conversation might naturally take off from the mutual reveal of job title, profession, or company affiliation. If not, then guide the discussion. Try questions that gather real information but aren't too personal. "Are you a member of this organization?" "Have you been to one of these events before?" "Do you know very many people here?" "Why did you come to this event?"

Do you keep your conversation focused strictly on business or do you bring up personal topics? One reason we take time for conversation is to make business more personal. I recommend not talking about sex, drugs, politics, and religion. It may sound old–fashioned, but you're trying to help other people like and trust you, and if you jump into one of those topics, you could alienate someone who would otherwise be a good business partner. Get to know each other first and the friendship can survive diverse opinions.

Don't be afraid to talk about business. That's why you're at a business-networking event. You can talk about your business, why you're in that industry, how long you've been in it, and how you help your clients. Even better, ask the other person about those topics. It's a process of discovery, not merchandising.

Most of us have no idea that the most important part of small talk isn't talking at all; it's listening. Your goal for small talk is to learn how the other person might be helpful to you and how you can give value to him or her. If you do all the talking and don't give the other person the chance to answer questions or tell his or her stories, you won't learn anything useful.

Think about the last time you met someone new and you had a great time. The person seemed to be so interesting and the conversation was terrifically engaging. Guess who probably did most of the talking? Next time you meet someone new, give the person the opportunity to feel that great about you, by being an active and careful listener.

> *Networking is a process of discovery, not merchandising.*

Meet People Recap

> *"Let us always meet each other with a smile, for the smile is the beginning of love."*
>
> — Mother Teresa

The secret to meeting people is to network with like-minded people. Not people who are the same as you, but people who are like-minded, in that they believe in networking on purpose. It makes meeting new people as easy as sticking out your hand and saying, "hi."

Meeting someone in person is only one way to expand your circle of contacts. You can:

- Send a letter or email to introduce yourself.
- Make a public announcement at an event.
- Use social media sites.
- Ask a friend or colleague to introduce you in person or on social media.

It is more important to get the card of someone you have built a connection with than to pass out your card to everyone within arm's length. Elevator pitches should be used for group introductions, not to sell your product to someone you just met.

Networking is a social activity. Social skills are *skills*, not talents or inborn abilities, and everyone can learn them. The most important social skill is making other people feel comfortable and that you are interested in them.

Be aware of and always work to improve:

- the first impression you make
- your manners
- your conversational skills
- your ability to listen more than you talk

Small talk is under-rated as a networking tool. It's never a waste of time when you:

- give someone the opportunity to get to know you
- learn how you can help someone
- give another person a positive experience
- share ideas or information with someone else
- find out what you and another person have in common

Meeting new people becomes easier when you know how to make it simple and what to do next. These are not talents, but skills that can be developed with practice and planning.

Get more ideas on how to meet people at www. theNetworkingMotivator.com

Who are you ready to meet?

Chapter 5

Stay Connected

"Make new friends, but keep the old;
one is silver and the other gold."

— Girl Scout song

Most of us will admit to being dismal at follow up; we all lose track of people in the busy whirlwind of our life. We let chance dictate whether or not we connect again with those who matter. You have only half the puzzle when you're willing to go places and meet people. The exponential returns come from these last two of the Five-Part Networking Success Plan™: stay connected and give value. It takes only a little more effort to consistently stay connected. If you do, you'll be in the top 10% of all networkers.

We build strong relationships over time. People don't remember you or what you do the first time you meet them. It's not until they've seen or heard from you several times that you begin to matter to them. It takes time and repetition to build the familiarity that is the base for building trust. If they don't see you or hear from you, people will think you moved away, went out of business, don't like them, you're not interested in them, or that you died. Even worse, they probably won't think about you at all.

If we know how much it does for our life and our business, following up will be our first priority. We'll have a system in place to keep track of who we know, how to reach them, and remind us to connect with them regularly

If you stay connected, you'll be in the top 10% of all networkers.

The purpose of networking is to put yourself in a position to give and receive value. We can receive value through our physical position. Show up, tell people what you do, and if they need what you have, you have a new client. It happens, but not nearly as often as we all wish it would. You will not be successful if they think of you only when you're standing in front of them.

Regular interaction with people is required if you want to stay on their mind. You can't call them every day but you can be visible, leverage technology, and use social media to show up in their environment as often as possible. When they think of something related to your business, your service, or even your passion, you want them to remember you.

Networking on purpose is a way to market yourself. If you don't have money to spend on advertising, all you have is your ability to stay connected with people to show them your value—to build connections and make a lasting impression on them. Networking on purpose means that every impression you make is valuable to the other person. When you talk to someone, send a message, or share something of value with someone, you send a clear message that *that person* is important.

Staying connected can also replace a portion of your sales activities. Staying connected shows others that you're willing to invest in them and their business; that you're looking for more than a quick sale. General marketing wisdom says you need seven touches over eighteen months to register on the consciousness of others. Every time you see or interact with people, you move closer to doing business with them without having to make a single sales call. You can send easily ignored sales messages or you can build the relationship. Staying connected through networking is the answer to "we're happy with our current provider." Be visible and memorable and they'll call you when that "current provider" drops the ball.

Even when you know all these benefits, staying connected is difficult to do. Why do you lose contact with people or neglect your new connections? It's easy to be casual about staying connected because negative things don't happen when we don't do it. Instead, nothing happens. It's hard to notice "nothing happening" when there are so many other things demanding your attention.

Staying connected contributes to the growth of our network and the development of trust. It contributes to our marketing, sales, and advertising efforts. It even makes us better people. Studies show that people who have more close friends and more social interaction are happier and healthier.

You don't have to be pen pals or "best friends forever" with everyone you meet. Find ways to strengthen your relationships and keep them alive in your mind and theirs. Remind people of your existence, acknowledge your relationship, and deepen the bonds between you.

One at a Time

"Reach out, reach out and touch someone. Reach out, call up, and just say hi.

— Bell Systems commercial, 1979

My grandmother was a terrific networker. I'm sure she didn't think of herself that way. I wish I had told her, but I was too young to realize it until after she was gone. She believed in the power of community and in people working together. She was involved in one of the biggest events that put her city on the map. She met or worked with nearly everybody who was anyone. Her greatest strength, though, was staying connected to people.

This was before everyone got his or her grandparents set up on email. She did it the old-fashioned way—by making phone calls and sending things through the mail. Grandma was in contact with family, friends, and former co-workers on a regular basis. Her network ranged from people she had worked with in the 1940s to the children and grandchildren of her friends who had passed away.

She got dozens of birthday and Christmas cards every year until she was well into her 80s. My brother once asked her why she got so many cards. She said, "You have to send cards to get cards." And she never missed sending a card or note for someone's birthday. Her newspaper was full of holes from clipping articles to send to people. She had a big, heavy Bakelite rotary phone that she finally wore out. And she went through reams of stationery. My grandmother maintained hundreds of relationships throughout her life by staying connected with people, one at a time.

We're in the digital age and we have technology that our grandparents could not have dreamed of. We have instant access to people around the world. We have the capability to send thousands of cards and emails with one click. We can make hundreds of phone calls using automation.

These are strategies that have their place in a well-rounded marketing plan. They serve a purpose in your networking plan if you combine them with the personal, one-at-a-time approach. You can do more to move a relationship forward with one personal touch than with ten generic ads. Interact with one person at a time by giving people something they need.

Cards and Letters

There was a time when going to the mailbox was a chore and getting email was a thrill. What's old is new again. We dread getting emails and real-world letters are fun. Tangible beats electrons. If you still read paper magazines, rip out articles and stuff them into an envelope for people who would like that information. It'll stand out in their pile of bills and junk mail. Send a greeting card. No one prints an email and props it up on the desk, but a card will sit there for days and remind someone of you. The cost of postage is tiny compared to the value of what you've done.

Email

Despite the growing tide of spam and commercial messages flooding our inbox, a well-crafted, personal email is still a good way to stay in touch with people. You won't always receive the quickest response, but most of us eventually read a message that comes from a real person. The odds that the recipient will read the email will be better if you told him or her to expect to hear from you. Use email the way a letter used to be treated—as important but not urgent. Take time to craft your messages so they are easy and interesting to read. Good grammar, correct spelling, and the proper use of capitalization go a long way toward making your messages sound intelligent. Put as much thought into the subject line as you do the rest of the message. It will be the reason your email gets read...or not.

Text Messaging

Text messages are opened and read more than 90% of the time, *if* the recipient has a smart-enough phone. Teenagers prefer texts, but not everyone is on board. Check before you text someone because it can be disruptive. Most of us can't resist the lure of a new message. Don't assume the recipient will recognize your number. Write your text in the form of a mini-email: "Hi Bob, is there a good day and time for you to meet me for coffee next week? Beth" Whatever you send, make it important and very short. We expect a text to be something requiring a quick response or from someone we want to hear from. Don't disappoint by sending a commercial message.

Reach Out and Touch Someone

Between texting and tweeting, we almost forget that a phone can be used to make a real call. Pick it up and use your voice to reach out and touch someone. It doesn't have to be an informational call. You can just provide encouragement or a word of thanks. Say something nice and then, "That's all; I don't want to take up too much of your time." You can call when you know the person won't pick up and leave a voice mail message that can be listened to more than once. I keep several nice messages in my voice mailbox.

Social Media

Facebook, LinkedIn, and Google all give you the opportunity to stay connected because of one-to-one messaging, and you can easily see what is meaningful in the other person's life. In addition to broadcasting thoughts and information with posts, use social media to show people you are paying attention to them as individuals.

- Post a thank you or a compliment directly on someone's wall for everyone to see.
- "Like" good things that happen to others.
- Express sadness and condolences for bad things.
- Share others' causes.
- Retweet the smart or valuable tweets of others.
- Comment on the Facebook, LinkedIn and blog posts of others.

- Write a referral for others on LinkedIn.
- Add people to your inner circles on Google+.

Drop In

An unannounced visit can be a great way to build your relationships. The difference between being a pest and being a welcome break from paperwork is to be quick and to bring something of value with you. Have a reason for stopping by and be respectful of the other person's time. Follow the lead of hotel marketing people. They are great visitors and always have a gift: a mug full of candy, fancy pens, or news of a big convention group coming to town.

What could be your purpose for dropping in? Cookies are usually welcome, although many offices have a love/hate relationship with them. Pens, pencils, and other logo items are appreciated and they stick around. I make personal visits to invite people to events. You could do the same—and the event doesn't have to be one of yours. The important thing is to make it a visit and not a sales call; if you're dropping off a brochure, it's a sales call.

Coffee Meetings

Meeting in coffee and tea houses to discuss life and business has been a tradition around the world for three hundred years. Ask someone to meet you for coffee when:

- he or she could be a great referral partner
- you want to learn more about what the person does
- you see someone you know but haven't talked to in a while and you need to catch up
- you can help someone with your knowledge or experience

Do you want to pick someone's brain? Most people are happy to give advice for the price of a cup of coffee as long as what you're asking for isn't what they do for a living. They're happy to talk to you about what they're capable of doing for you. But you wouldn't take your car to the mechanic and pay with a bagel or ask your doctor to diagnose you over coffee. Every professional has stories about being cornered at a reception or party to answer a "quick question," Or being invited to coffee and then asked to provide a full hour of consulting. Tell the person exactly what's on your agenda and stick to it during your get-together.

If you've asked someone to meet you for coffee just because you found him or her to be interesting or likable, keep in mind that you're still building a business relationship, unless you *do* have another type relationship in mind. That's a whole other book and I can't advise you there.

Sign Up Together

Invite someone to take part in an event or activity with you. You'll stand out and show people your commitment to building a relationship. No one will think you are silly or that it's immature. I run with business friends about once a week and regularly invite people to join us. Everyone is glad to be asked, even if they can't participate. You'll be pleasantly surprised at the positive reaction from people when you invite them.

- **Play Golf or Take Lessons** Unlike almost every other form of civic, association, and community participation, golf participation has increased in the last 25 years. Men still outnumber women four to one, and most new participants are older, but golf is still one of greatest business/leisure activities. With over a million golf tournaments and organized outings a year, there are plenty of opportunities to play. If you don't play golf, invest in lessons. Even better, take lessons with someone else to share the pro's time and build your relationship. Or team up to join a group such as the Executive Women's Golf Association.

- **Walk in a Fund-Raising Event** This is a great option if you don't play golf. You still get a good walk, but you don't ruin it with the golfing. Even the smallest cities have a regular number of runs and walk-a-thons. Sign up and then invite one or two of your connections to join you. You'll have the chance to converse in depth and show your willingness to invest time, effort, and money in helping the community.

- **Attend Church** If you're not religious, you might find the idea of inviting someone to attend church a strange suggestion, but churches of the 21st century have become community and activity centers in addition to being places of worship. You can find churches where the dress is casual, there's a coffee bar in the lobby, and professional musicians play live music.

- **Watch Sporting Events** Local sporting events, from college teams to AAA baseball, are accessible and inexpensive. I have a friend who buys season tickets for his family of four each year. As a business owner, he knows he won't be able to attend every game and that he can give the tickets to employees and key clients, or take people with him to the ball game when the rest of the family can't attend.

- **Arts, Crafts & Technology** I have a friend who supports her craft habit by bringing together women for an evening of greeting-card-making, using her tools. I've made new friends, strengthened relationships, and tapped into my artistic side. You can find classes at craft and hobby stores for just about anything, from cake-making to acrylic painting. If crafts aren't your thing, wait until your friend or co-worker buys a 1962 Olds fixer-upper. The get-togethers might be less formal and have fewer cookies, but the same ability to connect is there.

Stay connected one person at a time by doing something with that one in mind.

Each of these ways to connect one-to-one takes time and effort, but the return is much greater than the investment. This is good news if you aren't interested in crowds; you can build a network without going to big events. You can learn more in an hour-long coffee meeting than you could in a year of cocktail receptions. You can do more to move a relationship forward with one per-

98

sonal touch than with ten generic ads. Interact with one person, meet the person's individual needs, and let him or her respond. Stay connected one at time by doing something with one person in mind. Make it *personal*, not personalized.

Be Seen in Public

> *"I'll be seeing you in all the*
> *old familiar places."*
>
> — Frank Sinatra

You're going to be frustrated if you go to networking events to get immediate sales. Instead, you will always be successful if you go to stay connected to the people you know. Going to events to stay connected with people you know is an easy strategy that uses your time efficiently. It's simple and easy to do if you know why you're doing it and how to get the most out of your appearances. The more people there are at an event, the more opportunities you have to give and receive. The larger the event, the greater the opportunity to be visible and to connect. Don't worry about having to talk to everyone or be the life of the party. You can be successful just by showing up when most people don't.

Organized networking events are easy and efficient ways to connect with quite a few people at one time. How much time it will take and how many conversations you will have depend on whether the event is agenda or non-agenda. Events such as mixers, receptions, and open houses have a starting time and an ending time, but no set schedule in between. There might be an announcement or a door-prize drawing, but otherwise everyone is on their own to mix and talk to whomever they like. You control how much time you're going to spend at the event and can casually meet the people near you, or search around if you want to talk with someone specific.

Agenda events are luncheons, seminars, association meetings, training events, and leads club meetings, which have a schedule of specific activities that take place during the event. Free time may be limited. At first glance, agenda events might not seem as useful for connecting with people because there's less time to walk around and visit. This is true if you go to the meeting, walk in, sit down, talk to the people sitting on each side of you, listen to the speaker, and then get up and leave as soon as the event is over. Take the extra time and effort to meet new people and see the people you know. You can:

- arrive early and stay late
- volunteer to help with the event planning, set-up or management
- take a leadership role in the organization

Getting there early and staying late is good if you have the time. A better strategy is to volunteer to help the organizer of the meeting or event. Don't show up the day of and ask, "What can I do?" Call ahead of time to say you're willing to help. You could also give suggestions on what you're good at, such as set-up, reminder calls or greeting people at the door. If you're at the check-in table, you'll see almost everyone who attends.

Volunteering is a great way to feel more comfortable. You have a job, so you won't have to worry about what to say. People will assume that you know what's going on. Few things are better for a case of nerves than to have something useful to do. The most important part of volunteering is to show up. There's nothing worse than offering to help and then not showing up. When you make the commitment, make every effort to be there.

Joining an organization gives you access to all the other members. You can meet them either at the luncheon table or through a determined campaign of calling them one by one for a get-together. If it's a very large organization, you could find yourself working for years to get to know a significant portion of the membership. But if you take a leadership position, you'll launch yourself into tremendous visibility and credibility. The rest of the members will assume that you know what you are doing. They'll feel as if they already know you before you've even met. You'll put in extra time on the responsibilities of the position, but it's worth the greater visibility and credibility.

Social Media is Public

Using social media is a powerful and easy way to stay connected with the people you meet, online and in person. You are all there to be seen, at least by your group of friends and connections. Staying connected on Facebook is a function of commenting on, liking, and sharing other people's posts. On LinkedIn, try the group discussion forums, where you'll find people who have the same interests. Google is all about sharing information that's relevant to your circles of friends.

As with the things you say in person, make your social media posts positive. People, potential employers, and future clients will judge you by what you say on Facebook and Twitter. Assume that someone who matters to you could see everything you post.

Complaining sounds even worse on social media than it does in person. Instead, ask for help, advice, and input.

If you are using social media to build your professional network, keep it clean. Reveal personal preferences and hobbies strategically. Share information that is useful to the people you've met at networking events. Make your posts engage, entertain, or educate your viewers. If the business ideas and information you share on Facebook bores your family and personal friends or if your business contacts are seeing more than you want them to, there is an excellent alternative.

Keep your personal profile strictly for family and close friends. Tighten down the privacy settings and post whatever you want. Then create a Facebook page (not a new profile) and give it your name. Whenever you get a friend request on your personal profile, let them know that you are using it only for close family members, and invite them to "like" your page where you talk about topics that are mutually interesting to you both.

Twitter is smaller than Facebook, but it's another outlet for staying connected with your friends, followers, and fans. It's used more by "super users"—people who are on social media multiple times per day. The benefit to Twitter is that you need only listen to people who can add value to your life, whether it's by entertaining or educating you. The only people who will follow you are those who are interested in you.

Google+ allows you to create categories of people who will see what you're sharing. In other words, you can have a list of people who share the same interests and only they will get your posts about knitting. Or dirt bikes. You can selectively listen to only the people you choose to add and you can share only with those who are interested in the topic.

Leverage Technology

"Any sufficiently advanced technology is indistinguishable from magic."

— Arthur C. Clarke

As your network of friends, contacts, and connections grows, staying in touch with all of them in a meaningful way becomes more difficult. Research suggests that our brains are hard-wired for stable relationships with about 150 people. If you have an average-size family, you could already have 40 or 50 people in your social network of in-laws, cousins, neighbors, teachers, children's friends' parents, etc. It leaves room in your head for about a hundred business owners, referral partners, clients, fellow association members, industry experts, local leaders, and other important connections.

You need to have a good working relationship with more than a hundred people in order to be successful in your business. If you rely on keeping the people you know in your head, you're going to forget some of them. If you rely only on connecting with people one-on-one, you are going to run out of time in the day. You'll go a very long time between interactions. Expand your ability to connect using:

- Database-management tools
- Mass-communication techniques
- Social media lists

Database Management

You probably have access to a list of customers and vendors where you work; that's fine if they're the only people you want in your network. What about people you know outside of work? Or people in your association? Friends from church? Professional contacts outside your workplace?

Remember the days of the giant Rolodex? I always forgot whether someone was listed by first name, last name, or company name. I once worked in a company where the CEO had five of the giant-size, full-circle versions on his desk. I wondered how he kept track of who was in there.

You probably have bits and pieces of your network in a variety of places. A customer list at work. A small Rolodex at home. Association membership lists. Even your social media accounts are a type of database. You also have a giant pile of business cards in a drawer somewhere.

> *Your ability to stay connected is only as good as your database.*

Get all your contacts into one place. Technology now offers you flexible, powerful, and searchable options. Your email software has a contact manager. Customer-relations-management software packages are available; some designed for specific industries. You can also find free or cheap databases online. Get a recommendation from Your Nerdy Best Friend (and mine) Beth Ziesenis at www.AskBethZ.com.

The important thing is to get all your contacts in one system; it's worth paying someone to do it. Your ability to keep in touch with people is only as good as your ability to remember who they are and how to reach them.

Mass Communication

Does it seem impersonal to send the same message to everyone you know? Not when you have their permission to share your ideas, information, or to give value. Not when you avoid the sell, sell, sell approach. Not if you use it to open the door to one-to-one communication or interaction.

People can use interesting and relevant information whether it's sent to one person or to many. Be careful, though. It's very easy to cross the line from mass communication to mass selling. Make sure that every message contains something of interest and value. Write from the perspective that this is your side of a conversation, which means there's an expectation of someone responding. To talk with many people at once you can use:

- An email newsletter
- Social media
- A blog

What makes all three of these valuable is that each one allows and encourages immediate feedback. That is what can make these tools more about networking than about broadcasting or selling. Treat it as a two-way street. You say, "Hello, here's what I think," and then you ask, "What do *you* think?" You speak to a mass audience where everyone can be part of the conversation.

Chris Brogan, blogger and co-author of *The Impact Equation*, is fantastic at this. He has a huge platform with tens of thousands of blog and email newsletter subscribers. He encourages responses and asks specific questions. Then he replies. Nearly every time. Even if it's a few words. That feeling of being heard and responded to—by both parties—is what makes this a good way to connect.

Facebook, Google, and LinkedIn posts and tweets on Twitter are mass messages. Make these a way to connect with people by posting things that encourage interaction. Questions, requests for advice, points of view, helpful links and even silly stuff will get responses. Reply to the responses. That's called a dialog and it's miles away from the idea of an impersonal message thrown out to an uninterested audience.

A blog is also a way to post a message visible to everyone that allows for a conversation to take place by using the "comments" function. Treat your blog posts as a way to share something useful that will encourage others to respond and participate.

Social Media Lists

Customize your mass messages by using "lists" on Facebook and Twitter, and "circles" on Google+. These are tools within your social media accounts that let you group the people you know. Facebook creates basic lists for you including "close friends," "acquaintances," and people in your local area. These aren't a bad place to start, although they reflect Facebook's formula and not necessarily your opinion of who needs to be on that list.

Make your lists meaningful. It helps if you target posts about local interest items so you don't annoy your non-local friends. You can share business information with your industry or organization friends, while leaving the personal items for your friends and family. It allows you to be friendly and connect with more people while you stay up-to-date with the people you really want to focus on. I have lists for industries, different organizations, how well I know someone, where they live, and even a list for people I learn from.

Start creating lists on all your social media sites. If you're a new user, it's easy to go back and put everyone on at least one list. If you've been online for a while, this is going to be a big job, but worth the effort. You'll be less likely to miss posts from important people in your life and you'll be heard more when you target what you say.

Begin with Better Connections

"Coming together is a beginning;
keeping together is progress;
working together is success."

— Henry Ford

The best way to stay connected is to build a better connection in the first place. If you get a good start to a new relationship, you'll find it's easier to be connected in the future. The other person will share the work of staying connected if you create a strong bond from the beginning. You make better connections to begin with by finding something in common with the people you meet.

What you have in common doesn't have to be rare or strange; it could just be something that you're both passionate about. It's always fun to find someone who is willing to talk at length about the same thing you're geeked out about. When you find something in common, don't stay at the surface level by saying, "Oh, I like football, too." Drill down to get to the most detailed aspect of what you both like. Find out why and how long it's been the other person's favorite. Is he or she a fan of one player in particular? Or the coach? When did the person become a fan?

If you love gardening and you meet someone else who gardens, that's good. It's even better if you both like something more specific or unusual. Share a passion for growing orchids or heirloom cherry tomatoes? You've probably created a long-term friendship. At the very least, you have a starting point for future conversations ("Any new varieties lately?") and a way to give value ("Here's an article I found about the orchid business."). Take stock of your interests, hobbies, talents, or passions. What do you do that you can share with other people who might have a similar interest? If you don't have any hobbies because you spend too much time on your business, here's a great excuse to do something fun in the name of business-building.

> *The best way to stay connected is to build a better connection in the first place.*

You take on a certain vulnerability if you like something that another person thinks is silly or a waste of time. Some people will give in to the temptation to show you how clever they are by not liking that boring subject or ridiculous fad. They may think it's only a statement about their own preferences, but what you hear is an opinion that *you* are stupid. Or boring. You feel validated when other people approve of your choices and you feel judged when they disapprove.

Keep this in mind when someone talks about something you have zero knowledge of or interest in. You can simply move on to another topic, or you can take it as an opportunity to learn something significant. It's okay to say, "I don't know anything about it. What do you love most about it?" Or "How did you get into that?" Give someone permission to talk about his or her favorite things and that person will always enjoy your company.

What seems like a search for something to talk about is really a quest for common ground with a stranger. The strongest connections are built by more than just *enjoying* the same thing; they're built by knowing what you're both *obsessed* with. It's an opportunity for discovery. Finding someone who enjoys the same things that we do confirms our good taste. It feels great when you learn that someone else likes to do or watch the very same thing you do. It gives you an instant feeling of validation ("Someone else likes what I like!") and of instant belonging ("We're fans together.") It makes us feel more confident and gives the relationship a strong foundation. When you begin with a deeper connection, you'll both find it easier to stay connected in the long term.

Stay Connected Recap

"Communication—the human connection—is the key to personal and career success."

— Paul J. Meyer

Networking on purpose will be successful because you will do the things others don't do. Following up and staying connected is the weakest part of most people's networking strategy. It is where you can make the greatest gains in the strength of your network.

Once you understand how important staying connected is to the future of your network and your business, you will make it a priority in your daily activities. If you are consistent, you'll be in the top 10% of all networkers and you'll be networking on purpose.

Stay connected with people one at a time through personal interaction. Send cards, letters, and emails.

Use social media to connect in the digital world. Find activities to do with them in the real world.

Get the most out of your networking event time by using it to stay connected with the people you know. Maximize your visibility by volunteering to help the organizer or by taking a leadership position within the organization.

Your ability to stay connected depends on remembering who you know and how to contact them. Create a database of everyone you want to stay connected with. Leverage technology to share information and open the lines of communication with big segments of your network.

Begin with a stronger connection by discovering your common interests. Make small talk an important time of discovery, whether it's your business commonalities or something more personal.

Staying connected takes time and effort. Building a relationship requires patience. The greatest rewards come though the relationships you invest in over the long term. Consistently network on purpose by building a habit of following up and staying in touch with people.

Get more ideas on staying connected at www. theNetworkingMotivator.com.

How can you stay connected with your network?

Chapter 6

Give Value

"You can have everything in life you want, if you will just help enough other people get what they want."

— Zig Ziglar

When people ask, "What do you do?" they really want to know, "What can you do for me?" They're hopeful, but not optimistic. If you can do something for them, they'll be delighted. They'll care more about what you do and then they'll be happy to do things for you.

Thousands of years of wisdom have suggested giving value and giving it first. For some, this is reason enough to give. You know that when you give, you always get something in return, even if it's just a good feeling. You're ready to find ways to give as much value as you can so you can receive value in return. If you believe in a dog-eat-dog world, giving first may be difficult at the beginning, but it's worth it in the long run because:

- It's good karma
- It's the right thing to do
- You're a person who leads by example
- It builds up your social capital
- It's recommended in every major religious book in the world.

Still not sure that giving value will help you receive value? Or afraid that you're going to be taken advantage of? Science backs up the philosophical side. The power of reciprocity is present in every culture in human society. Reciprocity is the desire, conscious or not, to repay someone when he or she gives us something. The holidays are a perfect time to see and experience the power of reciprocity. Have you ever received a Christmas card from someone who wasn't on your list? You put the person on your list because you felt obliged to return the favor. Do you keep a few extra gifts at home or the office for those unexpected presents? That's the power of reciprocity. We feel obligated when someone does us a favor and will do whatever we can to pay the debt.

Giving value also increases the overall generosity of the community. A study by James Fowler from UC San Diego and Nicholas Christakis from Harvard showed that one act of generosity inspired three more. And each of those in turn generated three more in a real-life "Pay It Forward." If your community, organization, or peer group becomes more helpful, you'll earn a piece of the value that's going around. Everyone gets a slice from a pie that doesn't run out—it gets bigger the more pieces are shared.

Is it right to give so you get what you want? Yes. It's the only ethical way to get something, outside of an agreed-upon exchange of value. Otherwise, you're left with stealing, theft, extortion, graft, or manipulation to get it. You can't give value with the expectation that someone is going to give back something immediately in return. That's a market transaction, which is fine if everyone agrees to it in advance.

It all starts with you, giving value to the people who are important to you and your network. There are thousands of ways to give value. A few cost money, time, and effort. Many of them are simple, free, and abundant. You must believe in always having enough to give without hesitation. Networking is the process of building relationships through the sharing of ideas, resources, information, and experiences. That is what you give. It covers everything that

117

could be of value to someone else. Everyone needs these things and few people have enough knowledge or time or money to access them all. Networking on purpose is giving value by fulfilling those needs so that you can receive value in return.

Become a Curator (Give Information)

> *"Getting information off the Internet is like taking a drink from a fire hydrant."*
>
> — Mitchell Kapor

There's no lack of information to give. We're all overwhelmed with it. A flood of opinions, ideas, and links is constantly pouring down on us. We don't need more facts, resources, and recommendations; we need pieces of it that have been screened and selected just for us. Wouldn't you like to have someone sort through information for you? Would you be appreciated if *you* were that person, finding the needle in a haystack for others?

Become a filter. Become a curator of information: someone who collects, evaluates, and shares information. Like the curator in an art museum, you are carefully selecting information that is the most interesting and valuable for your audience. When you're looking at websites, email newsletters, newspapers, magazines, and videos, scan for links and information that will be helpful and relevant for your contacts. Send a link or article with a note to say why you thought they'd like it.

Don't limit it to digital sources. Anyone can send a link (and usually does), but you'll stand out from the crowd if you send real, printed materials that you tore out of a magazine or newspaper. This is what my grandmother did. She never wrote any articles of her own and I can't imagine that she ever gave speeches, but she knew what her friends were interested in.

This is why we engage in small talk. This is why we make the effort to deepen the connection. This is why we go to the trouble of keeping a database of people's hobbies, interests, and needs along with their contact information. The more you know about someone, the more targeted—and therefore the more valuable—the information you can share with them. It doesn't have to be all about business. We appreciate information about our hobbies, our interests, and even our home towns, if we're far from where we consider to be home.

You may end up becoming a curator by accident. A friend of mine manages a computer-repair store, so he's obviously knowledgeable about computers. He's also very good with customers. One day a client mentioned that he was heading out to dinner, but didn't know where to go. My friend is quite the foodie, so he was happy to make suggestions. Ten minutes later they were still talking about restaurants.

As the customer left, he told Dan, "You're my restaurant guy." Dan is now a curator of restaurant information for that client. He's their expert on that topic. And he doesn't take anything away from his status in the computer business. People assume that if you're knowledgeable about one topic, you must know about others.

You can always start with information that can help almost anyone in business:

- a new business opening up
- information about an association or service club
- invitations to networking events
- articles about business trends
- social media how-to's and news

These should answer the big question business people have when they get involved in social media. "What do I post?" Since networking is not selling and social media is about networking, the wrong thing to post is a sales message. You'll find that new fans are slow in coming and existing fans will leave if they get too many sales pitches.

Sharing information is crucial. People will follow you online because they like you personally and because they get something out of it. Share information that makes them an insider, that makes them feel smarter and that makes them feel more comfortable with you.

Have you ever heard a mortgage broker talk about rates, points, and the alphabet soup of lending acronyms? It makes me not want to listen because I have no idea what's being talked about and I feel dumb. What if it was broken down into little, interesting tidbits and explained

> *Give to get is the only ethical way to get what you want.*

in simple terms or made me feel that I knew something most people don't? I would become a fan online and in person.

One of my favorite restaurants posts on Facebook about their drink specials, lunch ideas, and events. What I really wish they would do is explain what curry is. And how a tandoori oven works. And what's in those four condiment jars? Teach me about the culture and language of India. I would eat there more often because I would be more confident about ordering new things. And I would have a great time impressing my friends when I take them to lunch.

What if you're in a network-marketing company where you're selling exactly the same product as everyone else in your business? How do you distinguish yourself in a crowded market? By becoming a curator of information. Be careful about sharing detailed information on the products, which could come across as a sales pitch. Better to share information on the *problem* that your products solve. For example, if you have a nutritional supplement, share links and stories about:

- vitamin studies
- health breakthroughs
- nutrition
- recipes
- exercise tips
- success stories (everyone loves a happy ending).

You can see how this supports your business and helps your potential clients at the same time. What if you sell a service? You still have a great opportunity to share information related to the service. I have a friend who represents an identity-theft-prevention service. She collects articles on incidents of identity theft from newspapers and the Internet. She also knows personal stories that others have shared with her. She has become a resource to those around her for guidance and help on understanding the topic.

You can give out information without hesitation because there is a never-ending supply. It's not information that's helpful; it's carefully selected and filtered information. AllTop.com aggregates news by topic. You can create your own custom page to track multiple subjects from thousands of sources. Other news aggregators include Digg.com, focusing on technology and Mashable.com, focusing on social media. Create Google Alerts for your topics of interest. Whenever Google finds new information, you'll get an email. Be specific in your alert search phrase. Otherwise, you'll be flooded with information that's too general for your needs.

Share Your Expertise (Give Ideas)

"A man may die, nations may rise and fall, but an idea lives on."

— John F. Kennedy

You're an expert in something. You know more about at least one topic than everyone around you—preferably something related to what you do for a living. But expertise in one area makes people think you're an expert in other areas. If you're new to your industry, consider your hobbies and education. What is easy for you, but hard for other people? The ideas and knowledge that you have is a renewable resource. Sharing your expertise costs you nothing and you still have the original idea available to share over and over.

Don't worry about giving it away and not getting paid. Become an expert on the lifestyles of the people who are your best customers. The more you know about them, the more you can give them what they want. Become the world's greatest expert on your product and on the problem it solves. The more ideas you have and share about the problem and the solution, the more you're going to sell.

Even people who make a living by selling information give away their ideas. Check out Technorati, a blog-ranking site. Once you plow through the politics, you'll see tons of blogs where knowledge is freely offered by people who make a living from writing

> **Share information on the problem that your product solves.**

books, blogs, and educational programs. The most successful consultants, authors, and coaches give away an astonishing amount of content. It's built into their business plan. They recognize that you must find a way to give value to help someone get to know, like, and trust you enough to do business with you. If these successful people have enough to give some away, then you do, too.

Todd Schnick, owner of the Intrepid Group, LLC, is a marketing, sales, and business strategist. He is also a blogger, a speaker, and has published four e-books. Two of them are free and the other two (on Amazon) are 99 cents. (*Note*: I'm in his book *Kicking Fear's Ass* and you can download it at http://tinyurl. com/kickfear) Todd spends a great deal of time and effort in giving away information and sharing his ideas because it builds his business.

Ideas are the offspring of your personal creativity. You don't want to hoard them. The more you exercise your creativity, the more ideas you'll get. If you're not able to capitalize on a thought, share it and let other people create something from it. Your idea can inspire and motivate. Everyone benefits from the value of what someone else can do with your idea. Give your ideas away and they will come back to you in a stronger and more valuable form.

A perfect time to share an idea or your expertise is in a conversation when someone expresses a need. The only hitch is how to share that idea without telling people what to do. We all love to give advice, but we don't enjoy getting it. Especially if we haven't asked for it. Avoid saying "Here's what you should do." Instead try:

- I wonder if...
- What if...
- I never realized that...
- Have you ever tried...
- What happens when...
- You know what happened to me when I...

Tell stories instead of giving advice. A good story includes a conflict or dilemma that ends in transformation or a positive solution. A rambling monologue of your last trip to the car-repair shop is not a story. Start out with the conflict or problem: "My car was overheating in the middle of the freeway." Then share the solution. "But then I called Bob at the garage and it was a simple heater hose." To give value in the form of a referral to Bob, add, "I can get you his number if you want to have your A/C looked at."

Speak to groups that can benefit from your expertise. Service clubs meet every week. The program chair has the tough task of finding dozens of speakers every year for the price of lunch. Don't make them look for you; send a note to offer them your expertise. Speak to give value to as many people at a time as you can.

You put yourself in the position to multiply value when you speak. Your audience will talk about your ideas. They'll apply your concepts to their own industries and to their lives. They'll take action to benefit themselves, their company, and the community. No group should be exactly the same after you've shared your ideas with them.

You can build an audience without going anywhere. Write about what you know, post it or publish it, and you'll build an audience. Once something is written down, it can be shared over and over. Your one effort can benefit an unlimited number of readers. The new ideas that you create during the process are saved—unlike conversations, which are lost in time. When you write, you have the ability to craft something that says exactly what you want to say before you release it.

It used to be that only the chosen few were able to see their work published. If you didn't have a book agent or a job at a newspaper, few, if any, outlets were available for your great ideas, stories, and expertise. Today, the start-up cost is zero and start-up time is five minutes. Try these technologies to get your expertise in front of your network:

- **Blogs**: Wordpress.com is the best way to create and host a blog for free. Don't build it expecting to get thousands of readers and make a living off the ad clicks from that traffic. Write to clarify your thoughts, explore your ideas and to practice writing (especially for the first three months when no one will see it). Until you develop an audience, use the ideas that you create in the blog as the seed for other forms of content.

- **Article sites**: EzineArticles.com is the largest of the websites that cater to ezine and blog publishers. You write and submit articles that become available for others to publish. In return, they give you a byline and a link back to your website. You can be on multiple sites with one article. Publishers of every topic you can imagine are looking for original content to fill their blogs and newsletters. Your articles provide great credibility as well as a boost to your search-engine rankings. The reprint and exposure isn't limited to online forums. I've had articles printed in magazines and newspapers after being found on EzineArticles.com.

- **Ebooks**: Once you've been blogging or writing articles for a while, you might find that there's a theme to your writing. If that's the case, you can collect all that information, tie it together, and create an ebook. The beauty of ebooks is that there's no standard length and there's no need for a publisher. You write until you've told people what you want to tell them, then you can sell it or give it away, like my friend Frank Kenny with his book *The 7 Secret Laws of Society: Social Media Essentials & Strategies for Small Business and Associations*. (Get it for yourself at www.FrankJKenny.com.)

- **Video**: If you don't have time to write or if you want to add another channel for your ideas and information, consider video. People are watching hours of videos and many now prefer to get information in that form. In their book, *The Video Tractor Beam*, John Riding and Everett O'Keefe state that sharing helpful information through video creates familiarity and establishes you as an expert.

What do you write about? Your industry. Your hobbies. Your area of expertise. Write about something that you *want* to become an expert in. About the problems that your product or service solves. About the people who have those problems.

Write articles, white papers, e-books, blog posts (on your own blog and as a guest blogger), Facebook notes, and tweets. The book industry has undergone a revolution. CreateSpace, Lightning Source, and Lulu.com make it possible for anyone to publish a book. It doesn't have to be a novel, the final authority on the topic, or hundreds of pages. It only needs to be long

> *No group should be exactly the same after you've shared your ideas with them.*

enough to help people solve a problem and show-case your knowledge.

Time, Talent and Treasure (Give Resources)

"Give gifts, be generous.™*"*

— Frank Kenny

Resources are the stuff you need to get things done. Physical resources include such things as building materials or money. Human resources are people and their labor. These are valuable because they are limited. You only have so much time in a day and a limited amount of money to spend. There's an old saying in the non-profit world that you can give time, treasure or talent to a cause or—in this case—to your network.

I've already shown you what I think are two of the best ways to share your time and talent. Take time to sort through information to find what is useful to others. Your talent is multiplied when you write down your ideas and give them away. There is also a more tangible way to give value to others.

Give of your treasures. This is anything that can be purchased with money or that has physical worth. If you picture bags of money—sure—that would always be appreciated, but gifts don't have to be large or expensive to be valued. Make them thoughtful and useful or fun. You can have cool stuff imprinted with your logo if you have the money in your marketing budget. Or get creative and find other ways to show appreciation to your network, clients, and future clients, like:

- Logo items if you have the budget
- Business books (new or used) that you found helpful
- Magazine subscriptions, which you can find for every possible interest
- Executive desk toys are always fun
- Food, especially homemade if you like to bake

You can get clues from conversations you've had with them or if you've been in their office. Always give without the expectation of an immediate return. Anything you give has to be in good taste and appropriate to a business relationship

You can give great value and satisfaction to people by giving to the causes and charities that are important to them. This might mean buying cookies or candy bars from their child. There's a huge growth in the number of people walking, riding, and running to raise funds for research. Even if your contribution is small, your gift will be noted and appreciated.

Have you received a holiday card from a vendor or client stating that a donation was made to a cause on your behalf instead of sending you a gift? If the gesture fell flat, it's probably because the cause meant more to the donor than it did to you. If you're going to donate, make it meaningful to the person in whose name you are donating.

Buy a ticket to their event. Not only do you directly contribute to the financial success of something that is near and dear to their heart, but you also give them personally a great gift. They probably made a commitment to selling a certain number of tickets and they will appreciate your helping them fill that obligation. Plus, you get the additional benefit of a pleasant evening.

Do business with the people in your network. The smaller the business, and the closer the owner is to the sales process, the more valuable this is to them. I've used this method of giving to justify a hefty shoe habit for a number of years. And it's the reason my skin-care system is a hodge-podge. I do business with as many different people as I can. It can become complicated, but it's worth the effort.

If you can use someone's service or product, it's a great sign of respect and trust to do business with that person. It adds to the person's bottom line. It increases his or her client or customer base. And it gives you the opportunity to directly experience the person's service and product. You put yourself in the position to become an advocate and an ambassador for the person's brand. Assuming the person does good work and you know how to network on purpose, both of you benefit from building up the association between the two of you.

You can give an even greater gift by sending referrals, but not a feeble "Oh, you know who you should call," recommendation. A strong referral is one where you've laid the groundwork with your enthusiasm for another person's services. This is the warmest of warm calls when the potential customer is expecting and even looking forward to a call. Few sales close quicker than a quality referral from a trusted business partner. It takes practice and effort to keep yourself in the position to give value in the form of referrals.

- Focus on just a few contacts; too many options can be paralyzing. Concentrate on people you have personal experience with. Look for referrals for people who you know will follow up and take action with the referrals you give to them.

- Know how to recognize a good referral. Call the people you are focusing on. Tell them you are trying to refer more people to them. Ask them to clearly define a good referral. "Anyone" and "everyone" are not good referrals. A specific description makes it is easier for you to recognize who needs their product or service.

- Keep a visual reminder in front of you when you are talking with your contacts. Eight business cards will photocopy onto an 8 ½ by 11 sheet of paper. Use a business card holder. Make an Excel list of names, numbers, and what a good referral is for each person. Keep any or all of your resources open and with you as often as possible.

- Ask questions and listen for clues. When you're talking to your clients and other business partners, listen to their complaints. These can be an opening to providing suggestions.

- Be up front. Tell your new acquaintances and business clients: "I've referred people to a group of trusted businesses for a long time. I've found that my new clients or friends appreciate knowing who to turn to. May I send you a list of my recommendations? If you need any of their services, let me know and I will personally introduce you."

Instant Gratification (Give an Experience)

"I've learned that people will forget what you said, people will forget what you did, but people will never forget how you made them feel."

— Maya Angelou

Help people feel great about themselves and they will feel great about you. It is the least tangible of all the things that you can give someone and yet the most powerful. It's a gift they can't refuse. It's something that can change their day, their week, or the course of their life. In one conversation, you can have a new friend for life.

Everyone needs respect, validation, and appreciation, says Kevin Hogan, author of 20 books on influence, including the international bestseller, *The Psychology of Persuasion: How to Persuade Others to Your Way of Thinking.* We all enjoy knowing we are respected. We all want to have our thoughts and feelings validated. Everyone likes to be appreciated. If you want to influence the way someone sees you, focus on these important needs. How wonderful would you feel if someone told *you* this?

"It's nice to finally meet you, I've heard about the great work you do and really respect what you've done for your organization. It's wonderful to have such an excellent resource available for the community."

People decide whether they like someone within a few seconds. The good thing about giving people an experience is that you can do it instantly. They'll remember you forever if you do this. You can give so many things that make other people feel wonderful in just minutes.

- **Your presence**: It sounds like taking yourself a little too seriously, but consider the event organizers' perspective. They've worked hard and they want great attendance at their events. At the very least, you're a warm body helping to fill the place up. You might invite other people to come with you. You become an asset to the event when you network on purpose.

- **Your attention**: It's a precious commodity. We can go for days feeling as if no one really looks at us or stops to listen. Dale Carnegie said that the one crucial law of human conduct is to always make the other person feel important. Important people get seen and heard by others. Slow down and give someone your full, undivided attention. You receive value when you hear something important that you can learn from or help another person with.

- **A kind word**: Is it trivial? Remember the last bad day you had. Did it turn around when your boss told you "good job!"? Or when your co-worker gave you a compliment? If you don't have anything else to give to people, you can always encourage them. Too many people spend their time having to listen to others tell them what they can't do. Tell them that you know they can do it.

- **A compliment**: Sincere appreciation can serve as an ice breaker. I met Dallas Teague Snider because she said "I like your jacket." We struck up a conversation and found that we have more in common than good taste in outerwear. Comments on performance and accomplishments make people feel validated and appreciated.

- **A sense of belonging**: A quick way to make a friend is to help someone feel welcome. If you see someone at an event who looks uncomfortable, introduce yourself and include the person in your conversation. A sense of belonging is a basic human need. The fear of not belonging is what keeps many people from networking. If they are treated as if they are unwelcome outsiders, they'll never be back. By extending a friendly hand and pulling them in, you'll break the ice and give them the wonderful gift of belonging.

- **The sound of their name**: Want to know a trick that will make you the most popular person in the room? Remember people's names. The trick to this trick? Learning them in the first place. Too many people excuse themselves from developing this skill by saying, "I'm good at faces, just not names." That's a terrible excuse. Face recogni-

> *Help people feel great about themselves and they'll feel great about you.*

tion is hard-wired into our brains. We're born with the ability.

Benjamin Levy's book *Remember Every Name Every Time: Corporate America's Memory Master Reveals His Secrets* is my favorite guide to remembering names. His basic system makes sure we learn a name in the first place. Use his mnemonic device—FACE—to help you learn names:

F - Focus on hearing someone's name and on the person's face

A - Ask a question about the person's name

C - Comment on the person's name

E - Employ (use) the person's name in the conversation

Someday we'll have implanted scanners that give us a readout—like the Terminator's heads-up display—for everyone we meet. In the meantime, develop the habit of making the effort to learn and remember people's faces *and* names to give them the great experience of being known and remembered.

Give Value Recap

*"Too often we underestimate the power
of a touch, a smile, a kind word, a
listening ear, an honest compliment, or
the smallest act of caring, all of which
have the potential to turn a life around."*

— Leo Buscaglia

The purpose of networking is to put yourself in a position to give and receive value. It begins with giving. You must have the mindset to seek out and create opportunities to give value to other people first. The power of reciprocity means that you do not have to worry about receiving value in return.

You can give value in the form of:

- information
- ideas
- resources
- experiences

There are thousands of different ways to give value. What you give may not cost you a great deal of money or time, but may be tremendously helpful to others because of the time or effort or expense you've saved them.

Of all the things you can give, a positive experience is the easiest to share and one of the most appreciated. Everyone wants more recognition, appreciation, and validation. When you're networking on purpose, you will never get tired of giving these experiences to others.

Get more ideas on giving value at www.theNetworkingMotivator.com

Who can you give value to today?

Conclusion

*"Successful people are always looking
for opportunities to help others.
Unsuccessful people are always asking
'What's in it for me?'"*

— Brian Tracy

In a way, I wrote this book backwards. You expect to start with the most important things, but in this case each chapter and each part is more important than the previous. You should spend the least amount of your time on the first three parts; Believe In ___, Go Places, and Meet People. You need just enough belief to motivate you to get started and go enough places to start building the relationships you need.

Too many people get hung up on going more places and meeting more new people. They have handfuls of business cards, but little else to show for it. If you want to be successful, spend most of your networking time and effort on giving value and staying connected. Those are the actions that will build a strong network that will give you the most value in return.

I have an easy way to remember how best to invest your time. Make a "cheat sheet" that you can carry around as a reminder of where to spend your time for the best results. On one side of an index card, write the definition of Networking on Purpose:

> *To be successful, spend the majority of your time and effort on giving value.*

Networking on Purpose is the ongoing process of building long-term, mutually beneficial relationships through the sharing of ideas, information, resources and experiences.

Below that, write the Purpose of Networking:

To put yourself in a position to give and receive value.

On the other side, write the FivePart Networking Success Plan™ as a list, like this:

144

Believe in ___

Go Places

Meet People

Stay Connected

Give Value

Draw a big triangle over the top of the five parts, the tip should be just above "Believe in ___" and the bottom line should be under "Give Value." See how much wider the triangle is for each part as you go down from the top? Each one has a bigger share of the pyramid. That's how you should allocate your networking time. Giving value is literally the base— and the foundation—of your networking plan.

Giving and Receiving

My goal is to give you as much value as possible in as compact a book as possible. I've learned from behavior-change expert BJ Fogg that success in do-ing something or developing a new habit depends on three things: your motivation, something to trig-ger you, and how easy it is to take the action. As the Networking Motivator™, I've written this book to help you be more successful at each of these. Use Chapter 1 to build up your belief and find what moti-vates you. Like my Facebook page at www.Facebook. com/TheNetworkingMotivator to get daily tips and to connect with like-minded people who will encourage you. And use the five parts to make networking a simple and enjoyable activity using skills you build on a daily basis.

If you've received value, I would be grateful to learn how I've helped you. I would also be glad to answer any questions or help you with any networking challenges you are facing. Email me at beth@bethbridges.com

You'll find a down-loadable Five Part Networking Success Plan ™ cheat sheet and other bonuses on my website at www.TheNetworkingMotivator.com/bonus. I'll add more over time and you can get more bonuses by subscribing to my newsletter. There's a sign-up on the website at:

www.TheNetworkingMotivator.com/newsletter

If you're ready to get more out of your business life and your personal life, it's time to put more into your network. It's the only investment in your future that is guaranteed to pay a return greater than you put in. Remember that the sole purpose of networking is to put yourself into a position to give *and* receive value. I hope you've enjoyed receiving the value in this book. Now go out and give value to someone else!

Get Your Bonus Audio Now!

Your bonus audio includes exclusive interviews with a marketing and positioning expert, a content development expert, an international etiquette expert and more. Get the benefit of their perspective and experience with Networking on Purpose in their lives. Plus you'll learn the story of how I connected with Bob Burg.

Go to http://bit.ly/19rOnpI to instantly download your bonus or scan the QR image below.

Acknowledgements

Anyone who writes a book about networking has been connected to and received value from a lot of people. I am horrified at the idea of leaving someone out. If you've contributed and you don't see your name, you are still very much appreciated.

I especially appreciate these people for their unique and valuable contributions:

My husband J.D., without whom I would have starved to death, wearing dirty socks in a dark office piled with empty tea mugs.

Bob Burg, who was originally an inspiration and turned into a friend.

Robert Mano, who has given me so much value as a friend and mentor that I will be eternally in his debt (but who is also the kind of person who would never call for it to be paid).

Chris Palmer, who was the first to say, "Why don't you write a book?" and who then listened a lot while I worked out the ideas.

Frank Kenny, for being a great example both online and offline.

Damon Thomas of Pixel-Polygon, for my logo design .

Kimb Tiboni of Kimb Manson Graphic Design for the cover design.

Wayne Everett of Everett Photography, for the cover photos.

All the members of the Clovis Chamber.

Authors, speakers, and content-creators Melissa Tosetti, Jill Hendrickson, Denise Branco, Todd Schnick, Chris Brogan, Dallas Teague Snider, and James Malinchak for showing me how it gets done.

The Running Club: Brett, Dan, Lisa, Susan and Kayhan for clearly illustrating the value of a mastermind group in accomplishing what you want.

Susan Daffron and James Byrd of Logical Expressions. Without their IdeaWeaver software I would never have finished this book.

And of course, Mom, Dad, GG, my brother, nieces and nephew. Just for being family.

About the Author

Beth Bridges is The Networking Motivator™ and has attended over 2,300 networking events in the last ten years. As the Chief Networking Officer of a large chamber of commerce, she has interacted with tens of thousands of people in person and online. She created the Five Part Networking Success Plan™ when she saw new and experienced business people struggling to network effectively.

Beth shows people how to use this plan to build their own highly responsive and powerful network through individual coaching, keynote speaking, seminars and the Five Part Networking Success Planner. Audiences consistently rave about her high energy, encouraging and valuable presentations. She encounters people who, months and years later, are still using and benefiting from the concrete and actionable ideas within the plan.

Beth has shared her networking strategy with corporations, colleges and universities, and business associations. New business owners, sole proprietors, independent sales agents, corporate executives and managers, solopreneurs and network marketers have all benefited from this practical but powerful system. She trains individuals, companies, and organizations on using her deliberate, intentional and strategic system for networking on purpose.

Beth is widely recognized by chamber of commerce executives across North America as a leading networking authority. She is an Expert Author on www.EzineArticles.com with over two hundred published articles and is a Top Author in the Business Networking category. Beth is a Summa Cum Laude and Dean's Medalist graduate of CSU Fresno with a degree in Agricultural Economics. Beth has leveraged her in-person networking skills to build large social media networks on Facebook, LinkedIn and Twitter. Connect with Beth at www.Facebook.com/BethBridges, www.LinkedIn.com/in/BethBridges, and www.Twitter.com/BethBridges

Become a fan of the Networking Motivator™ and the Five Part Networking Success Plan™ on Facebook at www.Facebook.com/TheNetworkingMotivator

CPSIA information can be obtained at www.ICGtesting.com
Printed in the USA
BVOW05s1746240314

348597BV00001B/1/P